WHAT YOUR

DIVORCE
LAWYER

MAY NOT TELL YOU

The 125 Questions Every Woman Should Ask

MARGERY RUBIN
with SALLY SAMPSON

A FIRESIDE BOOK
Published by Simon & Schuster

New York   London   Toronto   Sydney

This publication contains the ideas and opinions of its author. It is intended to provide helpful and informative material on the subjects addressed in the publication. It is sold with the understanding that the author and the publisher are not engaged in rendering legal or financial advice. The reader should consult her own lawyer or financial adviser before adopting any of the suggestions in the book or drawing inferences from it.

No warranty is made with respect to the accuracy or completeness of the information contained herein, and the author and publisher specifically disclaim all responsibility for any liability, loss, or risk, personal or otherwise, which is incurred as a consequence, directly or indirectly, of the use and application of any of the contents of this book.

Names and identifying details have been changed, and many characters are composites.

 Fireside
A Division of Simon & Schuster, Inc.
1230 Avenue of the Americas
New York, NY 10020

First Fireside trade paperback edition August 2009

FIRESIDE and colophon are registered trademarks of Simon & Schuster, Inc.

For information about special discounts for bulk purchases, please contact Simon & Schuster Special Sales at 1-866-506-1949 or business@simonandschuster.com.

The Simon & Schuster Speakers Bureau can bring authors to your live event. For more information or to book an event contact the Simon & Schuster Speakers Bureau at 1-866-248-3049 or visit our website at www.simonspeakers.com.

Designed by Ruth Lee-Mui

Manufactured in the United States of America

10 9 8 7 6 5 4 3 2 1

Library of Congress Cataloging-in-Publication Data
Rubin, Margery.
   What your divorce lawyer may not tell you : the 125 questions every woman should ask / Margery Rubin; with Sally Sampson.
       p. cm.
   "A Fireside Book."
   1. Divorce—Law and legislation—United States—Popular works. 2. Divorced women—United States.—Handbooks, manuals, etc. I. Sampson, Sally, 1955– II. Title.
   KF535.Z9.R83 2009
   346.7301'66—dc22   2008050196

ISBN 978-1-4165-8401-8
ISBN 978-1-4169-8717-8 (ebook)

To my wonderful children,
Christopher, Ian, and Nicholas,
and their loving support.
I am truly blessed.

ACKNOWLEDGMENTS

To those who believed in me and encouraged me to continue my mission: Kate Ballen; David Patrick Columbia; Christine Chapman; Mark Hausner; Patricia Russo; Albert Sax, M.D.; and Laura Torbet

To those who have been my team in creating and developing this book: Michelle Howry, my editor, and Carla Glasser, my agent. To Sally Sampson, my coauthor, whose humor and patience I am thankful for.

To the attorneys who have been my guardians: Joan Ellenbogen; Shelah Feiss; Frederic Siegel; and Ronald Spencer.

And last but not least to my clients, whose questions and needs have been a great incentive to write this book.

CONTENTS

Contents

ONE

WHAT'S A DIVORCE COACH?

What You Don't Know About Divorce CAN Hurt You

Here's a statistic you may have heard before: More than 1 million divorces are granted in the United States every year. Sad, but not exactly earth-shattering news. But here's something that may surprise you—nearly 70 percent of those divorces are initiated by a woman, which means that every year more than 700,000 women begin the divorce process.

While divorce is difficult on all parties involved, it can be particularly devastating for women—financially, emotionally, and spiritually. And this is true whether she initiates the divorce or whether it's thrust upon her. Divorce can put a severe strain on a woman's finances (both

1

on women who work outside the home and on full-time mothers) and makes it difficult to keep her work life on track while at the same time keeping the rest of her life in balance (particularly since women are often the primary caretakers for the children). In this book, you'll learn how to protect yourself and your family during this turbulent time, whether the decision to end your marriage was one you made or one that was made for you.

Of course, all divorces are difficult. The breakup of a marriage becomes a jumble of confusion, loss, and pain. Intimate partners are pitted against each other. Wrenching decisions must be made. The division of resources is often catastrophic for everyone involved.

Many women have a fantasy that when their marriage breaks up, their soon to be ex-husband (or as our friend Nicole Van Borkulo says, their "*was*-band") will act fairly, kindly, and reasonably. Or that once their ex is out of their house, he will be out of their lives forever. This fantasy usually crumbles early on in the divorce process. That was certainly the case when my twenty-two-year marriage reached its end.

From Wife to Warrior

When my own marriage ended, I was utterly unprepared, a fact that's all the more surprising considering whom I was married to: a man who was one of the top divorce lawyers in New York City. For years, I'd watched from the sidelines as my successful, high-powered husband negotiated his clients' lucrative divorce settlements (or protected their financial assets, depending on whom he was representing at the time!). And although I heard stories from him about the ways divorce could turn former lovers into bitter enemies, I never envisioned it could happen to us.

But as our own marriage was swiftly and suddenly coming to a close, I found myself in a tough position: in an adversarial relationship with someone who had spent a professional lifetime in the trenches of matrimonial law. He knew all the ins and outs, all the tips and secrets of negotiating an advantageous divorce settlement, and I found him turning that same ruthless skill upon me. My husband and I were now at war, and I was on the defensive. I knew I had to take steps immediately to protect myself and get what I deserved.

In order to survive, I had to be prepared and informed: Preparation is protection. And one of the very first steps I took to prepare for my divorce was finding a good lawyer to represent me. I knew from the years spent at my husband's side that having a first-rate lawyer was going to be my shot at getting what I wanted, needed, and well deserved. My future standard of living, the financial well-being of my children, the amount of security I would have in the future would all be determined by my smarts in cooperation with my lawyer.

But finding a lawyer was not going to be easy, since my husband's smart and aggressive reputation in the field was well-known. He was one of New York's "killer lawyers," and I think many of his colleagues were actually scared to go up against him on such a personal case. One lawyer I consulted with actually called my husband to tell him I was considering hiring him, which I later learned was totally unethical. He broke the rule of confidentiality that governs the legal system, but I was too nervous and anxious to call him on it. I realized then that I was entering a system that had its own version of the established old-boy network. I was going to have to become an active, not passive, part of this process.

Which is why, once I hired my lawyer, I began working to assist him in the case. I realized that I couldn't simply rely on him to do all the work on my behalf, because nobody knew this marriage and my husband like I did. I put together all the financial records I could find—telephone bills, credit card bills, receipts, and tax returns. I wrote a biography of our marriage to help jog my memory and bring back dates, details, and significant events. I made a list of my contributions to the marriage, paying special attention to the financial ones. I had an idea about the types of questions my husband's lawyers would be focusing on, and I worked hard to anticipate and defuse any issues that might arise.

For me, being actively involved in the divorce had an

empowering effect on my mental state. I approached meetings with my lawyers ready to do battle: I was prepared with questions about how they intended to defend me and what they needed from me to make the process easier. My phone calls to them were brief and to the point (making their jobs easier and my legal bills more affordable). I answered their requests for materials quickly and on time. (They often wanted copies of documents, budgets, or responses to motions.) I requested copies of key correspondence between the legal teams, so I could stay on top of what was happening. And I asked other divorced friends about their experiences and what they felt they could have or should have done better during the process.

Taking this active role proved to be not just helpful—it was vital. With my husband's vast matrimonial law experience and his formidable reputation in the field, my legal team needed all the help they could get to stay on top of what proved to be a long and complex case. And sometimes, as hard as my lawyers were working, I had questions that they just could not answer, not out of laziness or neglect, but simply because they didn't have the time or expertise to address all of my concerns. So in effect, I became my own "divorce coach"—anticipating questions, doing research, and taking charge of what had been an overwhelming situation.

But in addition to assisting with the practical aspects of the divorce, I realized that what I really wanted to regain was a sense of control during this uncertain time. I was determined that I would not end the process claiming that I had been forced to settle by my lawyers. But at the same time, I was realistic enough to understand that divorce is a compromise and I would sometimes have to give in order to get. I learned to set my priorities, and I found reserves of strength and smarts that I didn't even realize I possessed. It took four painful, grueling years to resolve my divorce. Needless to say, I learned a lot—not only about myself, but also about the practical and emotional aspects of the divorce process. I knew how to research information and negotiate a workable child-care arrangement, but I also knew how to deal with that middle-of-the-night phone call from the ex or the thorny custody and financial issues.

Soon after the divorce word spread, and friends—and friends of friends—began to call me for advice. Based on my personal experience and on long, painstaking hours of research, I was able to show other women how to take control of the unsettling, slow-moving legal process, teaching them how to substitute strategic planning for emotional responses and how to anticipate exactly what would happen every step along the way. I wanted to help others who found themselves in the same situation I'd been in, and I wanted them to benefit from my hard-won wisdom.

I believe that to be taken by surprise is to be in denial. The divorce process is convoluted; many accusations get made that may have little basis in fact. This does not make them any less frightening or anxiety provoking. If you can anticipate the potential problems and be proactive in resolving them before they even happen, the process will be swifter, smoother, and you'll get a better result in the end.

In 1995, I founded DivorceSource, the country's first consulting firm specializing in the practical issues of divorce. My divorce convinced me that there are inadequate resources for those who need personalized advice and information to help them navigate through this complex and daunting process—and that sometimes a lawyer is not enough to get you through to the other side.

Let me be clear: I am not a lawyer. But just as a woman giving birth may want the services of both an obstetrician and a birth coach, so too can a woman going through a divorce benefit from a lawyer as well as a divorce coach. There are some things a lawyer can't, won't, or doesn't have time to tell you. And in a divorce, what you don't know *can* hurt you.

The Role of a Divorce Coach

But what does a divorce coach actually do? I try to take the mystery out of the process by focusing on the concrete (rather than the emotional) issues that have to be resolved during the divorce process. More often than not, a woman arrives in my office because her husband is leaving or has already left. She comes because her lawyer is pressuring her to make decisions. In nearly every case, she comes to me feeling rushed, trapped, and more confused than ever—unsure what her next step should be and feeling paralyzed in the face of pressing demands for action from her husband, her lawyer, and others. I remember that situation only too well. *What to do, what to do?*

The situations I'm faced with are varied. When Jenny hired me she was at a crossroads: She wasn't sure if she wanted to divorce or not, but she knew that once she started the process it would get messy, so she consulted me to be sure she understood everything that this step would entail. Margaret came because she caught her husband cheating and was looking for help finding a lawyer and starting the divorce process. Sharon called me when mediation fell apart and she realized she was going to need some support to get through her divorce proceedings. And Natalie called just before she signed her final agreements, to guide her through the complex final steps of her divorce.

Women need help with their divorces at different stages of the process—some women need help working through just a single issue that's particularly difficult, while other women meet with me weekly for months, even years to talk through not only the practical concerns but also the day-to-day emotional aspects of dealing with a marriage's end. My mission is to help my clients make rational and beneficial decisions at a vulnerable time. Decisions made during your divorce will affect the rest of your life. Learning to navigate your way through this process enables you to establish a new future and protect your health, lifestyle, and financial assets. When children are involved, the divorce process is even more complex and a good outcome more crucial.

Whether you have a lot of money or children and no matter how you choose to proceed legally—whether you mediate, collaborate, or litigate—the issues are always the same. The questions can feel overwhelming and endless, and even though questions lead to answers, answers lead to more questions. I'm here to guide you through that process.

My first task when I start to work with a new client is to get her history: What was the couple's courtship like? Their marriage? What qualities about her husband did she most/ least admire? One of my jobs is to clear out the emotional wreckage and have the client take a good, hard look at the human being she is moving away from. Once she sees him more clearly, we are able to better navigate from there.

My next task is to discuss the legal aspects of what's in store. I take the client step-by-step, helping her to understand what the law requires and entitles her to. We discuss the finances, ownership rights, child support issues, custody issues, and what happens during the divorce procedure and after. We talk about how to choose a lawyer, how to deal with him or her on day-to-day matters, and how to be an active participant in the case. We discuss the timing of the divorce proceedings from beginning to end. My purpose is to make my client as comfortable as possible with the procedure, the vocabulary, and the format. Remember, surprise is a bad thing when it comes to divorce.

Lastly we deal with the finances: I help my client access and organize her records, bills, investments, monthly expenditures—all financial matters.

Remember, I am not a lawyer; I am not a financial planner; I am not a therapist. I am a coach. I am a person who has been through the process and survived. In fact I did more than survive, I came out whole and I came out having learned a lot. In *What Your Divorce Lawyer May Not Tell You*, I've drawn from my personal experiences as well as those of my clients over the past years. Having this book in hand will empower you, prepare you, and save you time and money. You will know what to ask, what to expect, and what to demand. We'll get to the heart of the practical everyday issues you'll face as you prepare to end your marriage, such as health insurance, pension plan rights, and professional license evaluations, just to name a few. This book is a hands-on, practical, yet personal guide to the specific and thorny questions of a divorce, your immediate guide to the multitude of real-life issues you'll have to deal with. And please remember: Divorce laws vary from state to state. This book is intended to offer a practical understanding about the majority of issues that states address in a divorce dispute. Once you have a general grasp of the issues that may be in dispute in your case, you will have to consult a legal professional to evaluate how the law in your state applies.

Divorce is both a learning and challenging experience. It's a time when you will have to confront unpleasant things about yourself and those around you. It's a time that tests your strength, your commitments, and your emotional stability, but it's also a time to discover your capabilities. I have seen what women can do when they don't think of a divorce as a tragedy but as an opportunity. Divorce can be a learning experience that leads to reevaluating yourself. You will survive because everyone does. For me it was a time to regain my confidence and sense of self. It opened the door to a new mission in my life, leading me to develop DivorceSource. You, too, can take a lemon and make it into lemonade.

TWO

SHOULD I STAY OR SHOULD I GO?

Deciding If and When to End Your Marriage

Many women come to see me in a state of shock. Their husbands have just announced that they want a divorce, or they themselves finally realize that they want out of their marriage. Many women start out in a state of denial: "I never saw it coming," many of my clients say (sometimes even when they themselves are the ones who are initiating the proceedings!).

But divorce doesn't just happen overnight: It lurks around for a long time. When I ask clients to think about and describe the atmosphere in their marriage, I can often see their problems clearly. And sometimes in describing it to me, they do too. I ask questions: Is your husband present or always working/traveling/socializing with the boys? How well do you communicate with each other? How does your husband treat you? How is your sex life? Do you argue a lot? The answers always reveal the obvious signs of trouble.

As I continue to investigate what has gone wrong, I often get mixed messages. She has been unhappy for a long time, or is suspicious about cheating, but is determined to continue the marriage. One minute she's angry, resentful, and filled with venom, while the next she knows he's the love of her life and she's not ready for a divorce. When it's *your* marriage, it's not easy to recognize that it's been dysfunctional for a long time. And on top of all the confusion and loss, the fear of being alone can dominate the hope that all your anger, sadness, and problems will go away.

One of my first clients, Leah, did not want to deal with the wealth of problems that had been festering in her marriage. Leah was a strikingly beautiful woman in her forties, a respected freelance writer who generally worked from home. She was on a rare business trip and called home to talk to her husband, Al, early one morning. The first time she called there was no answer so she assumed— hoped against hope—that he was in the shower. The second and third time: again no answer. Her mind began to wander and she became concerned that Al had had an accident at home. She called Jan, her good friend and next-door neighbor, to ask her to check on him. Jan convinced

Leah she was being foolish and told her to check at his office later.

When Leah finally reached Al, she asked him where he had been so early in the morning. He said that he had put the telephone in his dresser drawer because he'd had a series of late night hang-up calls and didn't want to be disturbed. In the end, he said, he'd realized he had forgotten to take the phone back out and just hadn't heard it ring. Sounds reasonable, right? Except for one detail: When Leah returned home, she saw that the telephone cord couldn't possibly have reached the dresser drawer. She knew in every fiber of her body that he had lied. She came in to talk with me about the situation, but in that first consultation we really didn't get very far. Looking back, Leah admitted she wasn't ready to deal with the truth, so she very consciously chose to put it out of her mind until other things began to happen that she simply couldn't ignore.

Al began claiming he was in places he wasn't, took business trips that he clearly didn't need to take, said he had late night meetings at the office yet didn't answer her calls—all causing her to take notice. Several months later the situation culminated with him moving out of their home to have, he said, a place to think about their marriage. This time she was prepared for action. She came back to me, and we created a plan to move ahead with divorce. It turned out that Al had been seeing a colleague for some time. And once Leah realized this, she was ready to end the marriage.

Sometimes it takes a while to realize what you really want (or need) to do in a situation. Try to think of your divorce as a new beginning, one where you clear out the old and break new ground (maybe even literally).

That's what the questions we'll be investigating in this first chapter will deal with: figuring out whether you're ready to take the first tentative steps toward ending your marriage. It can be a scary prospect. But look at the examples you'll find here to see if any of these questions or situations sound familiar to you.

Q I've been unhappy for many years but keep trying to make my marriage work. How do you know when you're really ready to divorce?

A When you really decide enough is enough. I guess everyone has her own level of tolerance, but most women tell me they just wake up one day and they know. Sometimes there's a triggering incident, like Leah and the early morning phone call. But often, there IS no big event; nothing changes outside yourself. You just know. The day you decide you no longer want to be talked to in that demeaning manner/live with someone you don't respect, trust, or like/be ignored anymore or whatever your particular issue is—that's the day you'll stop fantasizing about divorce and begin to feel the power to move ahead.

Jennifer is a perfect example of a client who chose to

deny a marriage that wasn't working. Jennifer and her husband, Mark, were both successful attorneys with high-profile, high-paying jobs. He traveled incessantly for work, and they were both caught up in a life of acquisition—buying a new house, taking luxury vacations, entertaining lavishly, and generally avoiding private time together. One evening Jennifer called Mark at his hotel to discuss some critical questions from their contractor. She was informed that he had checked out two days earlier. The very next morning he called her from his office to say he was back in town but had gone directly to his office from the airport. She asked some wifely but strategic questions about his trip and decided not to reveal what she knew. Jennifer chose to use this as a wake-up call and to begin paying attention to his actions.

A successful marriage is an edifice that must be rebuilt every day.
—ANDRÉ MAUROIS

Q Divorce is a really scary prospect for me at my age. Is divorce really a winning proposition for me at this point in my life?

A No matter what your age, the answer to this question is: not really, and absolutely yes. Financially, the only "winning" in a divorce is getting what is fair and equitable. Emotionally and psychologically, if you are unhappy and you want out, then getting a divorce is a big win. But really, "winning" or "losing" are not words I apply to divorce. It is neither one nor the other. It's a compromise for both people that offers an opportunity to change a way of life (your marriage) that probably wasn't what you wanted or expected. Although the beginning is the most difficult, vulnerable, and anxious stage, time truly does heal most wounds.

I encourage my clients to learn about their rights and not to be fearful in exercising them. Women often spend a lot of time trying to figure out what went wrong; they beat themselves up trying to understand why this happened to them. The most productive step you can take is to focus on your legal rights. Today, with divorce so prevalent, there is nothing to feel ashamed about. While women have greater rights now than in the past, you must learn to be proactive in order to get what you are entitled to. Letting your lawyer or your estranged husband dominate the situation is not to your benefit. Be tough!

Caroline, a cardiac nurse at a major teaching hospital, finally learned to get tough during her divorce, but it wasn't something that came naturally to her. She had lived in a marriage completely dominated by Bradley, her husband, who was chief of cardiology at the same hospital and essentially her boss. Bradley made all the household decisions, and even though Caroline made a decent salary, he controlled the household finances and only gave her money when he chose. Caroline thought this setup was normal, because that's how it had always been with her parents. But eventually, Bradley's controlling nature in all aspects of their lives became overwhelming, and Caroline decided to end the marriage.

Even after Caroline initiated divorce proceedings, her husband still lived in their house and still paid all the bills (and still controlled the purse strings). It's an increasingly common situation with the clients I work with, especially during tougher economic times. Caroline's lawyer had convinced her that this situation, though less than ideal, was inevitable, and he told Caroline that the status quo would have to remain until the divorce was finalized. But between the sluggish proceedings and Bradley's ever-more-demanding financial stipulations, Caroline began to feel trapped and without any rights. She had little money, and Bradley's presence in their household only led to fights that her young children were routinely exposed to. The entire situation had been going on for more than a year, and no matter what Caroline requested of her lawyer he would say, "It's a slow process that takes time. I promise it will eventually end."

A friend suggested she consult with another lawyer, just as one would seek a second opinion from a doctor. She soon learned she was entitled to interim support (called *pendente lite*), and because of his threats in front of the children and others she had grounds to have him removed from the household. For the first time, Caroline was being encouraged to demand her rights. Armed with this knowledge about her rights, she confronted her lawyer and got his attention.

There's only one way to have a happy marriage, and as soon as I learn what it is I'll get married again.

—CLINT EASTWOOD

Q **I suspect my husband is having an affair—should I confront him?**

A Yes, but not at first. Don't confront him until you have solid evidence. Generally speaking, not many people admit to an affair if they think they can get away with lying about it. They either come clean of their own accord when they are good and ready or wait until they are found out.

My suggestion is to do a little detective work: Check cell phone bills, credit card bills, e-mail, pockets, and drawers. Call your husband's office at intervals to see if he's there, and check with his secretary or coworkers without making them aware you're keeping tabs on him. Keep a diary of where he's telling you he's going to be. Finally and most important, trust your instincts. Affairs are a major factor in many divorces. For many women, they are a form of betrayal that they cannot forgive.

Ruth, a very sweet, very grounded woman, had been married for six years when she realized that her husband, Peter, was using his dog-walking time to pick up women. Peter hadn't been keen on getting a dog, so when he started insisting that he walk their Labradoodle (a very cute cross between a Labrador and a poodle) both in the mornings and after work in the evenings, Ruth was confused. What she did not know was that their dog was an attention magnet. Everyone who saw the puppy stopped to talk and pet him. One afternoon on her way home from her run, Ruth noticed Peter deep in conversation with a woman—long and lean just like Ruth—while the dog stood by, ignored. Their body language indicated that this was more than a casual conversation. Ruth decided to become her own detective and leave for her runs just after Peter left for his walks. After several weeks it became apparent that he and the woman from the park were meeting on a regular basis. Late night hang-up phone calls began.

Finally, after several months she discovered an e-mail from the woman in the park to Peter, confirming Ruth's suspicions that something was going on. And when she confronted Peter, she had real evidence. He tried to deny his affair but wasn't able to in the face of the irrefutable evidence. Ruth wasted no more time: She filed for divorce that month.

Q **My husband admitted to having an affair (taking out-of-town vacations with another woman), but this was years before we eventually separated. Is it still relevant to our divorce?**

A If you decide to pursue a divorce, it is of the utmost importance to find out if your husband is or has ever used substantial amounts of marital money to carry on this affair and therefore deprived you of your financial rights. In some states, including New York and Tennessee, for example (where you can have fault, or blame in a divorce), affairs are grounds for granting a divorce. And in some states, the fact that he was using marital income can be a factor in the final financial decision. There is no question that your husband's affair is devastating to you and may be the significant factor in breaking up the marriage. But an affair is not, in most cases, a significant factor in dividing the assets—unless those same marital assets were used in the course of the affair. Even if some time has elapsed, it still may be possible (and relevant) to prove this.

The key thing that the courts will be looking to ascertain is whether your husband used marital money to set up this affair and in so doing denied your needs or those of your children. Put your efforts into collecting the paper trail: Collect credit card statements, e-mails, letters, cell phone bills, airline tickets, restaurant receipts, etc. Spend your money on copying them, which is a lot cheaper than hiring a detective and a lot safer than relying on a single copy!

David, a classically tall, dark, handsome salesman, traveled a lot and had an on-again, off-again affair for about a year. His wife, Daniela, a fourth-grade schoolteacher, was confused, bereft, and angry, and she wanted some sort of revenge, if only to have him slapped on the hand by the judge. When Daniela met with her lawyer, she spent a lot of time (and money) detailing David's infidelities. While her lawyer was sympathetic, she explained to Daniela that it wouldn't figure into their settlement unless he had spent substantial money on his girlfriend. Daniela found absolutely no evidence that he had paid for anything.

On the other hand, Olivia, a computer consultant, used her computer skills to discover her husband Gideon's longtime affair. Not only did she find restaurant and hotel receipts, she found receipts for jewelry and other gifts. These were totaled up and deducted from his share of their assets.

*I love being married. It's so great to find that
one special person you want to annoy
for the rest of your life.*

—RITA RUDNER

Q Should I hire a detective to find out if my husband is having an affair?

A While this information won't necessarily help you, either psychologically or financially, sometimes women (and men) need to know the truth and the details about their partner's infidelity. But remember, detectives are expensive, and the mere fact that your partner had an affair probably won't have any impact on the amount of child support or maintenance you are entitled to.

But often the rewards gained from knowing what happened are more than just financial. Some women think that using a detective and getting the information will help them get over their feelings about their husband, but it rarely does. On the other hand, for some women it provides closure, which they badly need. Just look at all the reasons you're considering making this investment—financially and emotionally—to determine if it's really worth the money and the anxiety.

Q **Do you recommend marriage counseling while investigating divorce options?**

A Not really. It might sound a bit harsh, but in my experience, by the time people get to the counseling stage, problems have been festering for years and years. In fact, many professionals say that once the seed of divorce is planted in the mind, it can take as long as six years to blossom. That was certainly the case with Kim and Christian, who at first glance appeared to be the ideal couple—they ran a successful Internet business, had two children on the honor roll, and even looked perfect together with their all-American blond good looks. But underneath their carefully honed exterior, they were miserable. After fourteen years of marriage, they agreed to try counseling. Kim was desperate to make her marriage work and was willing to cooperate, work hard at counseling, and most important, learn to communicate more effectively. Christian, however, used the forum to try to prove that she was to blame for all the discord. Ultimately, their counseling was unsuccessful and their marriage ended in divorce.

I've seen it often: Sometimes people go to counseling to get permission to divorce. At times, I have encouraged my clients to go to counseling as an opportunity to learn what grounds their husband will use when filing for divorce. This will often help to determine how contentious the situation will become, which can help you decide what kind of lawyer to select and what papers you should be gathering as evidence. You may also get some clues about whether there are other women involved.

Jan was street-smart and book smart but used to being pushed around in her marriage. After many unhappy years together, she and her husband, Roger, were in counseling during a trial separation. He said he wanted time to think and be alone. But when Jan called Roger's apartment one morning, a husky-voiced woman answered the phone. The woman pretended that she had just dropped by and made several excuses for answering the phone. Jan immediately called me: What should she do? She and Roger were ostensibly still in counseling, trying to work things out. So what should she make of this strange woman in his apartment at seven thirty in the morning?

We decided the best course was for Jan to keep the incident to herself and discuss it directly with Roger at their next counseling session to see his reaction. True to form, his first reaction was denial—he firmly stated that there had been no one in his apartment, and he claimed that Jan had called the wrong number. Then, once she showed him how it was impossible for her to have dialed the number incorrectly (she had called the preprogrammed number on her cell phone), he recanted, saying it must have been a neighbor bringing him coffee while he was out running. But why, Jan asked, would a neighbor pick up the phone?

This incident was the end of their counseling and the beginning of their divorce proceedings. The lies continued, and this experience showed Jan that Roger would lie as much as possible throughout the divorce process. And believe me, he did.

On the other hand, I often recommend individual therapy for my clients during this disruptive and confusing time. Remember, you have power only over yourself and not others. The entire mission behind my company and this book is to empower you, and therapy can be an excellent tool to accomplish that.

My parents only had one argument in forty-five years. It lasted forty-three years.
—CATHY LADMAN

Q I have been unhappy for a long time, I have talked about divorce on and off with my husband, and yet I am indecisive about actually filing. I am tempted

to tell my husband that I am going to go ahead and file, but is that a good idea?

A This answer varies from situation to situation, but my general advice is to be circumspect and not reveal your thoughts or intentions. This is a tough concept for many women to accept, particularly when dealing with the partner with whom they have shared everything for the past several years. But this is a habit you must break. You need to hold back the information from your husband at this time, or the result could be devastating for your financial and emotional well-being.

Jacqueline, a sixty-year-old homemaker who lived in New York City and had a summer house in Connecticut, told her accountant husband, Paul, that she intended to file for divorce. He begged her not to, promising to spend more time together, to spend more time with their children, to be a better husband. She believed him, and she decided to give him a chance.

At first Paul was wonderful—more communicative and more present. But eventually, they both let things slide back into their old routines, and they found that their happiness was short-lived. One day, Jacqueline was gardening at their house in Connecticut when she looked up to find a process server coming up the road. He handed her a piece of paper: Paul had filed for divorce in Connecticut, a no-fault divorce state, that turns out to have very old-fashioned attitudes toward women. Jacqueline was Paul's second wife; when they got married, he was already established as an accountant and was the owner of their Connecticut home. In a state tough on women's rights, Jacqueline was unlikely to fare well in a decision concerning the percentage she would receive of these assets. Paul was well aware of this and bided his time so he could file in Connecticut. Additionally, Connecticut divorce courts aren't bottlenecked like they are in New York City, and Paul was confident the process would move more quickly. As a result of her disclosure and indecisiveness, Paul had gotten a leg up.

Jacqueline had to refile for divorce herself, this time in New York, where their primary residence was located, and then prove to the courts that they didn't really live in Connecticut (Paul's business was in New York, he paid taxes in New York, etc.). They wasted their time and money—and, incidentally, the court's time (which judges don't like) based on Paul's sneaky move and Jacqueline's inability to make this gut-wrenching decision in spite of the fact that she knew—after twenty-four years of marriage—that Paul was unlikely to change.

This is not to minimize how hard a decision this is—getting a divorce is difficult under any circumstances, and many of us (rightfully) want to believe a marriage can be saved. The truth is, every decision you make along the course of a marriage and a divorce will be a judgment call. Know your spouse, know your marriage, and know your rights.

This was the lesson my client Mary learned when she came to me, unhappy in her marriage but unsure of her options. Shy, careful, and just a bit detached, Mary had been discontented for years but was intimidated by her husband, Jonathan, and wasn't ready to see a lawyer. She came to me in order to educate herself about the divorce process. If Mary could understand her rights, I believed, she would gain the confidence she was so sorely lacking.

After two sessions with me, during which we talked a lot about her relationship with Jonathan and how they connected to each other, she began to understand one of the key elements she was ignorant about: their finances. Jonathan liked controlling this aspect of their marriage, and Mary had gone along with him. When she signed the tax returns she never asked questions. He gave her a small allowance for household expenses, but she didn't see their investments or larger financial picture. I know it sounds impossibly old-fashioned, but these were two educated, modern, fortysomething adults (with rather retro viewpoints on marital finances).

So Mary began to take steps to change this. She took notice of the bills and financial papers around the house. She started to keep an accounting book, making note of her expenditures. She made copies of bills and bank statements. By the time Mary gained the courage—two full years later—to ask for a divorce, she knew where things stood financially, completely taking her husband by surprise. She was no longer the mousy woman who had walked into my office; she was in charge and prepared. I was happy to be able to have helped her, but remember: You don't need a coach *or* a lawyer to get knowledgeable about your finances. It's a right that every woman has and deserves.

All marriages are mixed marriages.
— CHANTAL SAPERSTEIN

Q **My husband and I have agreed to live apart for six months. We don't want to involve lawyers, because we want to think about what we really want to do about our marriage. He says he'll take care of the bills. What do you suggest?**

A I understand your reluctance to consult a lawyer: It's expensive, it can inflame the situation, and it feels like it will defeat the purpose of creating a nonadversarial environment. However, my advice is to consider your husband's character: Is he trustworthy? Does he live up to the promises he makes? Does he pay the bills on time? Will he question you or argue about what was spent and why? Trust your instincts.

That said, it is always advisable to devise a clear plan for temporary financial arrangements during a trial separation. This requires a full, detailed discussion, and I strongly suggest you commit your plan to paper so there is no chance of a misunderstanding. Together you can write, sign, and date the agreement. If you have trouble later and need the aid of a lawyer, you will have proof of your husband's intent and whether or not he defaulted on his agreement. If he does default, you could then establish his lack of credibility, which could be used against him during the divorce procedure. (From a purely legal standpoint, some states would not consider this agreement enforceable if he defaults because it is not court ordered. Do some research at your local library or online to determine what your rights are in your state.)

Brian, a surgeon, didn't want a divorce, nor did he want a trial separation. He wanted to stay married to Judi, a school principal, who earned about half the income he earned. Brian finally agreed to move out of their home and continue paying for the home's expenses while he and Judi went into counseling. They agreed, in writing, that he would continue paying the mortgage, utilities, and credit card bills. Brian kept his word, and it was clear to me that he did so because he thought the situation was temporary and that he would be moving back in. He kept his word, in part, because he was still trying to woo Judi, but he also proved himself to be a decent man who upheld his promises to his wife and family. While eventually their marriage did not last, they treated each other with respect throughout the process and ended their marriage amicably, due in large part to the clear, fair guidelines they agreed upon at the start of their separation.

Marriage is a great institution,
but I'm not ready for an institution yet.

— MAE WEST

Q Do you think it's easier to be left or to be the one leaving?

A Neither role is easy—the emotional stress on both partners is huge. It's impossible not to wonder whether you are doing the right thing. But I've observed that the ones who leave first have often been doing their homework. They've been consulting lawyers, finding out their legal rights, preparing financial documents, sometimes hiding money, redirecting income, and organizing an exit strategy. I've also observed that the one who is left has sometimes forced the other's hand—they don't have the courage to leave but don't want to stay in their marriage.

Jessie and her husband, Burt, both successful accountants who made identical salaries, had been fighting during their entire fifteen-year marriage—in fact, their daughter Rosette called them "The Bickersons." Burt finally got so fed up that he packed his things and moved out of their home. They were separated for a year, and during that time Burt gave Jessie a small amount of money for child support but didn't give her anything toward the mortgage, bills, or upkeep of the house. Jesse tried to reconcile, but eventually she got mad at his refusal to move back home and slammed him with a divorce and desertion order. Burt was shocked: What had he done wrong? He hadn't paid the bills, he'd been dating, and he wasn't helping out with any of the child-care duties, and yet he maintained that he just couldn't understand why Jessie had made this "rash" move. Jessie was the one who finally filed for divorce, but it was clear from Burt's actions that he wanted out.

Spouses who have been left may find themselves stressed by their very lack of preparation. Once you are notified by your spouse's lawyer of his intent to begin the action, you may feel pressured to find a lawyer immediately. I advise my clients not to buckle under the pressure but instead to take their time in choosing a lawyer in a reasonable time frame—a few months is not too long to take making this decision. Often it's in these early, tumultuous days of a separation that the big mistakes in strategy take place. Pressure to take action should not cloud your decision. Your lawyer must be your principal ally, and you must have confidence in his or her ability. It takes time and interviews with several attorneys to gain the experience needed to make a wise choice.

We were happily married for eight months. Unfortunately, we were married for four and a half years.

— NICK FALDO

Q **Is it more advantageous in a divorce case to be the defendant or the plaintiff?**

A For the most part, it doesn't matter. If your husband files you are designated the defendant and he becomes the plaintiff. Nowadays this designation is not meaningful. The only reason it would be to your advantage to be the defendant is in the unlikely event your case goes to trial.

The plaintiff presents his case first, which allows you, as the defendant, to adjust your strategy if necessary.

❧

Always get married early in the morning.
That way, if it doesn't work out,
you haven't wasted a whole day.

—MICKEY ROONEY

❧

Q My husband and I have been struggling for years. I have recently reconnected—and fallen back in love—with an old boyfriend. I know now for sure that I want out, and I've filed for divorce. My husband doesn't know about my new boyfriend; could that affect my divorce case?

A This is tricky on a couple of levels, and I'd advise keeping your new boyfriend to yourself as long as possible. Even more than any legal exposure this relationship might give you, making your new boyfriend public will jeopardize the possibility of your having a good relationship with your soon to be ex. During a divorce people are angry—often

irrationally so—and your husband's knowing about your
new flame will only serve to make the negotiations tenser
and more difficult. Whether you are discussing custody,
child support, or vacation time, your boyfriend will become
the focal point of everything. The business at hand is that
you want out of this marriage; you have to focus on that.
And by the way, reconnecting with an old boyfriend isn't
uncommon at all.

My client Nancy was on her second marriage and had
two young children, one with her first husband and one
with her second. She had been writing letters and e-mails
on and off to Donald, her college boyfriend, which her
husband, Ron, knew. Truthfully, Ron wasn't thrilled, but
he didn't want to be perceived as not trusting her or as
being too controlling; he thought—or at least hoped—it
was harmless.

Eventually, as Nancy's marriage to Ron deteriorated,
Nancy and Donald arranged to meet in person and began
an affair. When she decided once and for all that she wanted
out of her marriage (only in part to be with Donald), she
confessed everything to Ron. Ron literally heard nothing
Nancy said after that—he wasn't able to think about or
take responsibility for any of their problems because all he
could think about was Donald and how he had ruined their
marriage. Nancy's telling him made her life much more difficult and their divorce infinitely more painful.

Even before Nancy's divorce was finalized, her boyfriend left her. The end of her affair didn't change how she felt about her husband. She wasn't sorry to be getting divorced, but she was surely sorry she had told him about her affair. The breakup muddied the waters even further, making her husband wonder if she still wanted out. Nancy had to reiterate to her husband over and over that she still wanted a divorce, which caused even more pain for both of them.

As we discussed earlier, while infidelity may not be grounds in and of itself for divorce, if either spouse (you or your husband) uses your joint assets to pay for an affair, that may affect the financial settlement. These laws vary state by state, so check the laws in your area.

Whoever said "Marriage is a fifty-fifty proposition" laid the foundation for more divorce fees than any other short sentence in our language.
— AUSTIN ELLIOT

Q My husband just told me he wants a divorce; my life is a total nightmare and I am an emotional

wreck. I can't sleep, I can't eat, and I can't get any work done. One of my friends is urging me to see a lawyer immediately, but another said I need to take things at my own speed and chill out. What is your advice?

A Unfortunately there isn't a right answer to this one; it really depends upon your own level of need. Is this a threat or an actual declaration of intent by your husband? Couples often play this kind of head game with each other and in the end do nothing about it. Only you know how your husband will behave. If you can relax and not be too reactive, take the time to learn about your rights. Educate yourself, prepare yourself. Talk to people who are divorced, consult a therapist, read a book, surf the Internet, collect financial documents, and consider seeing a financial advisor to help you get a handle on your finances. I see many people play with threats of divorce when they are unhappy with each other, but don't take action.

It's not as great a day for the bride as she thinks.
She's not marrying the best man.

— ANONYMOUS

Q My husband and I have discussed everything and are in almost total agreement. Is it naïve to think that a divorce can be amicable?

A As a rule, yes, it is naïve. However, there are always exceptions. Money is usually the most heated issue, but if you feel that the realities of your financial situation are completely out in the open, then the two of you should have an easy time organizing your divorce settlement. It depends upon what "almost total agreement" means. You need to know what the outstanding issues are and whether or not they are deal breakers for you. If you really are "in almost total agreement," you are in the perfect situation to use mediation to dissolve your marriage (see chapter 3).

Other than dollars, I find the house is often one of the biggest obstacles in reaching or breaking apart an agreement. The attachment to the living environment is very strong for many women, perhaps because it's the place they spend the most time and the place they feel most secure. Additionally, many people—including therapists and lawyers—feel that children need to stay put in order to minimize the coming upheaval in their lives. A home is generally the major asset in a relationship, representing a large sum of money for the parties to divide.

Sam and Judy were able to resolve the issues of the house through their ability to talk to each other. Judy had never known what it was like to live in the same place for long. She was born into an army family, and moving from base to base had been her way of life. She felt it was important for her children to have the stability of a familiar place and to avoid more upheaval. Fortunately, she was able to express her feelings to her husband and he was willing to listen. Their major problem, common in many households, was that their house represented the major asset. After much discussion and thought a compromise was reached: Judy would stay in the house until Tommy, their youngest child, reached high school. That was four years away. At that time she would sell the house and they would split the proceeds. It was a good solution for their family, and it allowed for some continuity in the present and some security for the future.

However, I often warn people to consider their overall financial condition if they decide to stay in their house. Sometimes without the sale of the house you can be left cash poor—meaning you have a major asset but are left without enough money to support your day-to-day existence.

Ending a marriage is one of the most important decisions you'll make in your lifetime. It will not only affect you but also all the others who surround you. Getting a divorce should never be a knee-jerk response to an on-the-spot crisis but instead must involve a well thought out evaluation of what you want and what you expect from your life. Too often women think of themselves as second-class citizens and are willing to settle for less than they want, need, and deserve. The changes in women's rights and independence outside our homes have not, unfortunately, changed enough of our attitudes. Don't be afraid to recognize your unhappiness and use that recognition to empower yourself to move forward.

THREE

HOW DO I HIRE A LAWYER?

Navigating the Most Important Relationship
of Your Divorce

Your lawyer—and your relationship with your lawyer—
is a key component in determining the outcome of your
divorce. While your lawyer will be your employee, he or
she will also be your partner and your guide through
this challenging time. But not all lawyers are created
equal.

Despite the title of this book, I do think highly of lawyers and I believe they're the cornerstone of the team you'll
need to get you through your divorce. But I also have seen
how mystifying and complex the legal system can be and
how widely the quality of legal representation varies. The
bottom line: You cannot assume you will be taken care of

by your lawyer. You absolutely must take the time to read and research and to ask questions on your own. Lawyers and mediators are a necessary part of the legal process, but if you expect your lawyer to be your friend and confidant you are starting with a mistaken premise. Never forget that your lawyer is running a business—and that his very expensive hourly fees add up quickly.

This chapter will help you better understand what to expect from your lawyer (professionalism, responsiveness, information), what not to expect from your lawyer (a shoulder to cry on, advice about your life choices, patience for repetitive questions), and how to be a responsible participant and your own best advocate during the legal process. I encourage you to ask questions, get organized, and be realistic about your expectations. Make your meetings with your lawyer productive by being prepared and taking notes. Don't let the final decree be one you feel was dictated by your lawyer. Be a participant. Gather the information about your finances, lifestyle, and needs for you and your children so your lawyer will have the tools he needs to see that the end result is equitable.

Remember that your lawyer is not your therapist, parent, or best friend. Lawyers are there for the purpose of getting a job done, and your constructive input is needed. Here's how to help them help you.

Q Should I tell my lawyer everything?

A Yes. Everything you tell your lawyer is confidential; he needs to be aware of all the facts. You don't want to set the stage for mistrust, and you don't want your lawyer unprepared for something your husband may bring up.

Marion was a stay-at-home mom; her husband, Joe, had recently changed careers and was receiving an entry-level salary, and he was cheap with what little he had. When Marion began to contemplate divorce, she started to take out a small amount of cash every time she went to the grocery store. When she filed for divorce she didn't reveal her hidden savings account, which held several thousand dollars. Somehow Joe discovered it and told his own lawyer, who then brought it up in a session with the judge regarding temporary support.

When Marion's lawyer later presented the bank statement to the judge, showing cash on hand that was nowhere to be found on any of her financial disclosure papers, the judge was not pleased. Marion had been a stay-at-home mom: How, the judge asked, had she accumulated this sum? The judge requested a full accounting and asked the couple to return to his chambers at a later date. In the meantime, he refused to rule on any of the issues before him. He also wanted a documented breakdown of Marion's monthly budget to see if her financial requests were on target. In the end this incident set a negative tone for the rest of the negotiations, with all parties—including Marion's lawyer—suspicious of her veracity.

Had Marion told her lawyer about the secret savings account, her lawyer would have insisted she disclose it but could have likely turned it into a positive (she was frugal and could be responsible with money). Not only did the lie cost her more money in delays and legal fees, it cost Marion her integrity and her credibility in the courtroom. Once a judge thinks a party is lying about one thing, he will not trust them about anything. This is very important—you must disclose everything to your lawyer and to the court. Let the lawyer worry about putting a good spin on how you got the assets.

Q How do you choose a lawyer? What criteria do I use to judge if this is a good lawyer for me?

A The first and most important criterion is that your lawyer specialize in matrimonial law. You need a lawyer with considerable experience in handling divorces. Do not, under any circumstances, hire a generalist who handles divorces on rare occasions, no matter how much you like or respect her. A brilliant business lawyer is not necessarily a brilliant divorce lawyer. It's a bit like going to a great obstetrician when what you need is a cast for your broken leg.

How Do I Hire a Lawyer?

Check the reputation of all recommended lawyers through friends, other clients, or on the Internet. Make note of education, age, and participation in county divorce programs. And in addition to the professional accolades, take note of your rapport with this person—after all, you'll be spending a lot of time together over the coming months. Does your lawyer take the time to explain things clearly? Does your lawyer listen well, hear and understand your questions and concerns? Is your lawyer a litigator? You need to know this in case you have to go to trial—although most divorces never do. At the same time, it's important to find someone who is the right fit for you and your case. Sometimes you need the most experienced name in the business—the "killer attorney" who has an established reputation in your area. However, the downside is that he may not have the time for you. Sometimes you just need a good, experienced attorney who will pay close attention to your case and not hand it off to an associate. Look at your situation and think about what your needs are.

If you are not happy with your attorney's work, you must speak up, early and firmly. If she doesn't change her behavior, then it's time to change lawyers. If she does, you have saved yourself the effort of making a change. You don't want to have to change your lawyer midway through this process if you can avoid it (though you should if you are truly unhappy with her work). But doing your home-work beforehand and working closely with your lawyer as an active partner in your case will help you determine early on if the working relationship is a good fit. Ultimately, you have to feel comfortable and confident in your own ability to choose whom you will hire.

Not long ago Lara came to me because her lawyer's attitude was troubling her. Lara, a tall, physically imposing but fairly meek woman, had moved out of the home she shared with her husband, Morris, an exacting engineer. Lara and Morris were communicating only through their lawyers, and she asked her lawyer to request that she have use of one of the two family cars. Lara's lawyer said it was unnecessary for her to have a car and told her he knew what was best for her—as if she were a child making unreasonable requests. Additionally, she had noticed that she was being billed for correspondence between the lawyers and the judge and requested copies. Her lawyer told her his secretary would send copies of the correspondence. After several months and more requests, plus bills for additional correspondence, Lara had received nothing except excuses. My advice was to leave this lawyer, since he was nonresponsive, seemed to have little or no respect for her, and was possibly overbilling her.

I've been married to one Marxist and one Fascist,
and neither one would take the garbage out.
—LEE GRANT

Q **I'm tempted to change lawyers midway through my divorce, but isn't that expensive? How do you know whether to grin and bear it or start anew?**

A Yes, changing legal representation midway through your divorce is an expensive proposition, and you have to be very clear about whether your own complaints are valid or not. I recently had a client who told me one of the more outrageous lawyer stories I have ever heard; in fact, it is so outrageous I had trouble believing it. Bobbi was a buyer for a large department store; she was a decision maker who was used to overseeing a large staff and had lots of responsibilities in her professional life. But throughout her marriage she had been bullied by her real estate lawyer husband, Dmitri. She came to me with a troubling story—she went to see her divorce lawyer, who told her that he had just returned from a successful meeting with her husband and his lawyer. Bobbi was shocked. She knew nothing of a meeting! How, she asked, could you meet without me? What right do you have to exclude me? He said they were all lawyers and "understood one another."

Bobbi left the office and pondered the situation. On the one hand, she was daunted by the prospect of changing lawyers in the middle of the process and having to start all over. But on the other hand, she knew this was absolutely wrong and her lawyer was not to be trusted. After a day or two her lawyer called her: He thought he could settle one of their sticking points, but he needed another meeting with her husband and his attorney. Bobbi said she would come to the meeting, but her lawyer replied that she would hamper the meeting and would be a detriment to the swift resolution of this issue.

She fired him, and she was right to. We came up with a strategy whereby she offered to pay him (minus the cost of his time for the meetings she had been excluded from) when her case settled. Her lawyer could have sued her for the money in order to get it sooner (her divorce took four years), but that wasn't in his best interests either (she didn't have money until her divorce was settled). By the time it came to pay the first lawyer, Bobbi was even clearer about how inappropriate, unethical, and unprofessional he had been and how poorly he had represented her in general. She probably could have filed a complaint against him— which might have caused him to be sanctioned, which he wouldn't want. She turned the tables and ultimately offered to pay him 25 percent of the bill; they settled on 50 percent.

Q Why do you suggest I write a brief biography of my marriage? How can it help me?

A The first thing I ask my clients to do when they hire me as a divorce coach is to write a mini biography of the marriage. I believe this exercise helps you to focus on the realities of your marriage—what went wrong, what went right, and what you can anticipate from your partner during your divorce. This biography can serve to clarify your relationship and bring forth some of the underlying issues that led to your breakup, sometime issues you weren't even aware of. Although this process can seem tedious and painful, I've found it to be an indispensable tool for organizing your thoughts in preparation for a meeting with a lawyer.

During your initial conversation with a lawyer, he will ask you for a marital history—an overview of the very same points you will have outlined in your marriage mini bio. It's often difficult to tell your story in a concise and informative way in your lawyer's office if you are anxious, nervous, or under a lot of emotional stress. If you have done your homework beforehand and gone through the process of writing a marital biography, you'll be prepared for this meeting (and make the best use of your lawyer's valuable—and expensive—time).

You should, of course, begin at the beginning: how you met your husband and what your courtship was like. Highlight the important and happy events in your life, such as your wedding, the birth of your children, special vacations, the purchase of your home, and career high points. List your conflicts, money problems, illnesses, behavior patterns, infidelities, problems with your children, your parents, your friends. If your husband was previously married, how well was that divorce resolved? More than likely he'll repeat the pattern. And the same goes for you: If you have been married before, disclose that as well and the details of that breakup. This exercise will probably be an awakening to patterns in your relationships.

Remembering how he treated you and how he treated other people in your lives will help highlight your husband's character, his values, his behavior. Marta, a tiny, almost childlike woman, chose to do her marital biography with a tape recorder instead of writing it down. With little effort she began to see patterns and issues in her marriage that had been going on for a long time. She remembered various events that had been long tucked away in the recesses of her mind.

Most significant of these was when her husband, Denny, a salesman for a pharmaceutical company, purchased a tiny weekend house. Marta had been left a small amount of money in her grandmother's will. Denny, desperate to buy this house, convinced Marta to use the cash for the down payment. Within a few years Marta became pregnant with their first child and decided to draw up a will giving their child a share in her property. Her share in the house was one of the items she wanted protected for the child. She discovered that she had no ownership in the house. It was listed as a property belonging solely to her husband. While the equitable distribution laws (see page 118) meant that she still had joint ownership of this property (since any property acquired during a marriage is considered to be owned by both parties), it was a major betrayal of Marta's trust.

Finally the incident was forgotten, but many years later when Marta began to write her marital biography, she recalled the incident and his harsh denial that he had done anything wrong. Over the years they had any number of arguments concerning money. Her husband's attitude was that whatever he earned belonged to him—and what she earned also belonged to him. True to form, the money issue was a major problem during her divorce.

Q What issues should I be thinking about when organizing my marital biography?

A Thinking about and writing about your marriage is one of the best exercises you can do to help you confront the reality of it. However, many of my clients find it daunting to discipline themselves to confront their marriage. Some people find it easy to write, while others prefer to tape-record their story; either way, this assignment is guaranteed to bring clarity to your understanding of the marriage. This is also an excellent tool to clarify what things about your relationship you need your legal counsel to know. Here are a few issues and questions to keep in mind as you sit down to undertake this exercise:

- Your courtship and plans you discussed (How did you plan your marriage? How did you initially envision your life together?)
- The beginning years (How did the wedding go? How did you work out problems at the start of your marriage?)
- Changes in your lives (Were there any issues involving jobs, moves, parents, health, or children? What were the financial or emotional effects of these?)
- Your lifestyle over the years (Did one of you spend while the other saved? How did you spend your money? Did you agree on your financial priorities?)
- Household responsibilities (Were chores divided equally? What type of work around the house did each of you undertake?)
- Financial highs and lows (Who made the decisions? What did you each earn? Who actually paid the

bills? Did you have separate bank accounts or joint?
Who filed the taxes?)
- Your social life (Did you share the same friends?
Was one person more social?)
- Your relationship history (Do either of you have a
previous marriage and/or children from a previous
relationship? How was that situation handled?)

Not so long ago, Michelle appeared in my office determined to get all the information she could to go up against her husband, Jack. She now realized that the anger Jack expressed about his first wife and children was about to be focused on Michelle and their own children. His withholding of money, complaining about the ex-wife's handling of the children, and general animosity toward them was about to happen again. As I often told her, people don't change, and Jack would create his own truths about who was at fault. It was my job to help her select the right attorney and help her to organize her information so that she would feel more confident and secure going forward.

Q What information about my marriage and what
records, bills, and documents should I bring to an
initial interview with a lawyer?

A Your first meeting can be upsetting and anxiety provoking, so I suggest you bring all the material listed

below to your first consultation. It is highly unlikely that you'll get to all of this information in the initial meeting, but it will give you an outline to follow while you're discussing these issues with your attorney. There's a lot you'll want to say in this first consultation, but remember to leave time for your attorney to speak, too. Bring:

- Your marital biography (see above)
- The names and ages of spouses and children, if any
- The length of your marriage
- Where you were married
- How long you've lived in the state
- A short summary of who is seeking this divorce and why
- Your work history and income
- Your husband's work history and income
- Copies of any financial papers such as stock accounts, tax returns, bank accounts, any appraisals. If not available, write an overview of what you own: property, art, antiques, cars, etc. Make copies for your lawyer, and always keep the originals yourself.
- A general budget/estimate of your family's monthly expenses
- Questions you want the lawyer to answer (see page 59)

How Do I Hire a Lawyer?

Ask your lawyer when you set up the appointment whether he would like you to send any of this information beforehand. Sometimes, it helps him to get a sense of you and the case to see this material before the meeting, and every bit of preparatory work the lawyer can do will potentially save you money. Other times, a lawyer prefers the first meeting to be "clean," or free of preconceived ideas and information. It's up to you and your lawyer.

During the meeting itself, remember to take notes and listen carefully so that when you interview other lawyers you will be able to compare what was said. Some experts recommend tape-recording your session, but you have to inform your lawyer first. If your lawyer says no, get another lawyer. Keep in mind that lawyers are salesmen. Proceed with caution. You are interviewing the lawyer, not the other way around.

Before you make your initial appointment, find out what the lawyer's fees are. I can't emphasize this enough. Judith had quite a surprise on her first interview with a potential lawyer. An associate joined them for the consultation, and when Judith received the bill, she was alarmed to find out that both people had billed for their time. I encouraged her to call and question the billing. The lawyer told Judith to pay what she thought was fair. I thought this was very manipulative of the lawyer and suggested she not choose him. In the end, the lawyer eliminated the associate's time from the bill and told Judith just to pay his fee.

Q Should I expect to pay for an initial consultation with a lawyer?

A This varies, but whatever the law office's policy, it should be clear from the beginning. Ginny and Jorge went to see a mediator who offered—as many mediators and lawyers do—to conduct the initial interview free of charge. After an hour in which they were making a lot of progress, the mediator asked if they wanted to continue. They said yes and kept talking for another hour. They left thinking they would hire him. A week later they received a bill for the additional time. They were shocked. They understood that they had benefited from the additional time but felt that the mediator should have been much clearer about his fee structure and should have specifically told them that the second hour would be billed. Because of how poorly the mediator handled this situation, they decided not to hire him (and, incidentally, they negotiated that bill and paid only for half the second hour's fee). Ultimately, they felt that he was not straightforward and that their working styles weren't a good fit.

How Do I Hire a Lawyer?

*Women who marry early are often overly enamored
of the kind of man who
looks great in wedding pictures and
passes the maid of honor his telephone number.*

—ANNA QUINDLEN

Q What questions do you suggest I ask when I interview lawyers?

A Below is a list of questions you might want to choose from to ask a lawyer in your initial interview. Since the interview usually runs one hour, edit your questions and give him a chance to give you an impression of himself and how he works. Focus your questions on fee structure and give him a brief overview of the reason for your divorce and the financial situation. Let him take over the interview from there. If you decide to hire him or if he's a close possibility, go back to resolve the unanswered questions before you finally retain him as your lawyer. Important questions to ask include:

- How much do you charge? Is it hourly or a set fee?
- What is your retainer fee?
- What other expenses do you charge for (faxes, phone calls, postage, travel time, copies)?
- Are court appearances charged at a different rate?
- Who will work on my case and how much do you charge for each of them? (Ask to meet the associates if you decide to retain the firm.)
- How long do you think the divorce will take?
- How do you work? Will you work with me throughout the case? When does the associate deal with me? Is there a paralegal and what are her responsibilities?
- What kind of settlement do you think I'm entitled to?
- Do you do the litigation yourself?
- Do you handle divorce only?
- What is your financial expertise? Are others involved?
- Tell me about other cases you consider successful.
- Do you know my husband's lawyer and what do you think of her?
- Do you represent more women than men?
- What do you think about the judges in the matrimonial courts?
- Can you give me a brief overview of the judges sitting on the bench?

- What can I expect in child support?
- What are my chances for an equitable outcome?
- What law school did you attend and how long have you been practicing?
- What was the hardest case you dealt with? What made it hard?
- What issues in my case could be difficult? (Complicated issues pertaining to business evaluations, searching for sources of income, child custody, and abuse are just some of the factors that could make a case more difficult to handle.)

When angry, count to four; when very angry, swear.
— MARK TWAIN

Q Do you suggest I bring a friend or relative with me to the initial interview?

A It is not unusual to want this, and good lawyers will be comfortable if you bring someone to your consultation. It's very important to check on this before your appointment. Most important, choose someone you feel comfortable sharing your personal and financial issues with. If possible, take someone who's been divorced, since she will be more familiar with the situation. She may help you be less anxious and more confident. It's another pair of ears and someone to take notes for you.

Lauren brought her sister Molly to her first consultation with her lawyer. Molly took notes, asking questions from time to time. Later, when they discussed what had been said, Lauren was shocked to discover that she had spaced out through most of the conversation. Luckily, she was able to recollect most of it by reading Molly's notes.

But remember: When you meet with a lawyer alone, everything you discuss is confidential. The presence of a third party breaks the confidentiality of the entire meeting, which means both the lawyer and your friend are under no obligation to keep quiet.

Q A friend of mine just got divorced and recommended her lawyer. But she has some real complaints about her final settlement. How do I know who is the right lawyer for me?

A When selecting a lawyer, it always helps to have recommendations from people you know and trust. That said, you should interview several lawyers to get a sense of their personalities, styles, their overview of your case, and the ways in which different lawyers treat you. As far as your friend is concerned, she may be a person who won't be satisfied with any settlement. What are her complaints? Do her complaints sound reasonable or petty? Get very specific—interview her in the same way you'd interview a lawyer. Find out how and why she chose that lawyer in the first place. Did she feel her lawyer was honest and kept her apprised of what was happening? If the lawyer was a man, what was his attitude toward women? How was the billing handled? How much direct contact did she have with her lawyer? Was she charged for the initial consultation, and if so, how much? My advice would be to use her complaints as questions in your interviews with other lawyers to see how valid her discontent is. Unfortunately, there is no way to absolutely guarantee that you are making the right choice.

The problem with marriage is that it ends every night after making love, and it must be rebuilt every morning before breakfast.

—GABRIEL GARCÍA MÁRQUEZ

Q What is a mediator, and when is a mediator a better choice than a lawyer?

A A mediator is a trained professional—a lawyer or therapist—who is familiar with the legal aspects of divorce.
His priority is to resolve conflict and keep the peace, but it
is not his job to decide what is fair. His job is to guide you
toward an equitable solution by offering guidance in helping you make decisions. This is wholly different from the
job of a lawyer, whose job it is to advocate for you, to get
you what you want, fair or not.

When you use a mediator, the three of you—you, your
husband, and the mediator—work together to draw up an
agreement you and your husband can live with. Of course,
this requires that both you and your husband feel trusting
and comfortable with your choice of mediator and, more
important, with each other. Mediation allows you to be in
control of your decisions rather than have a judge imposing his decisions on you. Upon completing mediation,
each of you must consult with your own lawyer to review
the final agreement and to verify that your legal rights
have been protected. A formal document is then filed in
the courts. For the most part, you will be able to eliminate
the stereotypical divorce lawyer, who sets up an adversarial
situation.

A mediated divorce takes less time and money than an
adversarial divorce. Mediation averages between five and

ten sessions; payment can be by the hour or sometimes a flat fee. Although I recommend you get referrals from friends, you can also consult your state's Council on Divorce Mediation.

Jackie came to see me a little over a year after she caught her husband Burt cheating on her. She had spent that year working on her marriage but eventually deemed it hopeless. Although she was very hurt, she was ready to move on. Burt, on the other hand, was not happy to have been "caught" and wasn't ready to move on. They agreed to see a mediator, and after three sessions they were just a few steps from resolution when the process came to a halt, with Burt storming out. Jackie decided she'd had enough and got her own lawyer, who had been on the sidelines, involved. Since their agreement had been almost complete, things moved very quickly from there.

Marriage is like a cage; one sees the birds outside desperate to get in, and those inside equally desperate to get out.

—MICHEL DE MONTAIGNE

Q Do you recommend mediation?

A In many cases, yes. Mediation is a way for both you and your husband to resolve your differences without hiring individual lawyers and using the court system. Together you have the power to create the agreement that governs the dissolution of your marriage, including issues like marital property and debt, child and spousal support, and child custody and visitation, including how you make decisions regarding your children. In an open session, you, your husband, and the mediator meet together and focus on specific issues and on what you are trying to accomplish. There is an open and free exchange of information, which allows you to understand the situation and negotiate the resolution together. It's often a much more economical solution, because it takes less time.

Kate and Walter described their marriage as very argumentative, and in private, each described the other as someone who had to have his or her own way. When they decided to divorce, they both immediately chose their lawyers and diligently began the process of dissolving the marriage. After nine months and an endless exchange of paperwork between the lawyers, nothing had been resolved. A good part of their savings account had been depleted in legal fees. This served as a dose of reality for them, and when they began to talk things out with each other, I recommended that they use a mediator.

Ultimately they realized that mediation was the quickest and most civilized method to resolve their disputes. The mediator was able to keep them on track by explaining the legal aspects of their actions while helping each spouse to see the other's perspective on issues. For the first time they were working together to negotiate an agreement that they both felt comfortable with. In fact, they were learning how to talk reasonably and respectfully with each other. Fortunately this was carried through in their dealings with each other regarding issues about their children. After ten sessions, they had an agreement.

It's important to remember that you have some flexibility with mediation. If it isn't successful—in cases where one spouse is abusive or intimidating—you can just walk away and continue the process through your lawyers. Mediation requires spouses to deal with each other as equals.

An appeaser is one who feeds a crocodile,
hoping it will eat him last.

—WINSTON CHURCHILL

Q What is the difference between mediation and arbitration?

A People often ask me this question. The simple explanation is that a mediator has no power to impose a decision. He or she is there to facilitate a resolution that both parties find acceptable. An arbitrator, on the other hand, is a bit more like a judge and has the power to impose a settlement after hearing both sides of the issue. However, arbitrators are not part of the divorce process but can be used in place of commercial litigation (a trial) in specific matters such as real estate, union/employee rights, financial partnership, and personal injury disputes. Many states encourage mediation in divorce because it is less costly than litigation and eliminates bottlenecks in the court system. Some states require it be attempted before a divorce proceeds to trial.

Q What is a Collaborative lawyer and how does this type of professional differ from a regular lawyer?

A Many lawyers say they are collaborative lawyers or work collaboratively. This is *not* the same thing as being a capital "C" Collaborative lawyer. Collaborative lawyers must be trained in the collaborative process, a dispute resolution model that has received a lot of attention and acclaim in recent years.

Collaboration is another form of dispute resolution you can use to dissolve your marriage. In a Collaborative divorce, you and your husband each hire your own Collaborative lawyer, who is specially trained in resolution techniques. You each meet with your own lawyers, but then all four of you meet and negotiate the terms of your divorce together. All participants agree to work together respectfully, honestly, and in good faith to find win-win solutions to the legitimate needs of both parties.

In the February 16, 2007, edition of *Forbes* magazine, writer Elizabeth A. Reingold tells the story of a couple who used Collaborative divorce to come to a mutually beneficial financial settlement. June and Sam had been married for twenty-five years, and the primary financial asset in the marriage was Sam's business—a business that was currently experiencing a downswing in value. The business's valuation was a concern for both of them—Sam was worried he'd have to sell the business in order to pay a financial settlement, and June knew that if he sold the business at this low point, it would result in less money for her.

Using the Collaborative divorce method, they came to an agreement that worked for both of them—June would maintain nonvoting shares in lieu of receiving alimony (because she believed that the business would eventually recover and give her a larger payout in the long term), and the arrangement allowed Sam to keep the business intact. According to the article, the business has continued to grow instead of being drained or dismantled, as often is the case for businesses bound to divorcing couples, and both parties felt comfortable with the decision they made.

Q What's the difference between Collaborative divorce and mediation?

A Collaborative divorce has much in common with mediation, but there are some key differences. In mediation, there is one neutral party who helps the disputing parties try to settle their case (and, typically, no lawyers for either party are in attendance). While the mediator helps facilitate a dialogue and guides the discussion, he or she cannot give either party legal advice. Mediation can be useful, but it requires a greater level of understanding and patience between you and your husband. If either of you becomes unreasonable or stubborn, if you are unable to negotiate fairly, or if you become upset, the mediation can become "unbalanced" and ineffective. If the mediator does not find a way to deal with the problem, the mediation can break down or the parties can be unhappy with the resolution.

In Collaborative divorce, both you and your husband have a lawyer by your side at all times, and it is a more structured (and usually more expensive) process. Each side has quality legal advice and advocacy at all times during the process. It is the job of the lawyers to work with their own clients if the clients are being unreasonable, to make sure that the process stays positive and productive.

Q What happens if you don't really collaborate?

A There is a built-in incentive to collaborate once both parties agree to a Collaborative divorce—namely, cost and time savings. At the start of the collaboration process both parties must sign a collaboration agreement, which states that neither party may go to court, or even threaten to do so, once the Collaborative process begins. If that should occur, the Collaborative law process terminates and both lawyers are disqualified from any further involvement in the case. Lawyers hired for Collaborative law representation can never under any circumstances go to court for the clients who retained them. If the process breaks down, you must, in effect, start from scratch. This is, as you can imagine, a powerful incentive to come to an agreement!

However, sometimes the process does break down. Wallace, an entrepreneur, and Deena, a massage therapist, loved the idea of having a Collaborative divorce. They picked their attorneys, met with them alone, and then met all together once a week for about two months. Deena went in with what I thought was a very fair proposal, focusing mostly on their children. Their assets were relatively modest, and neither made a large salary; there wasn't much to argue about. However, Wallace was out of control. He often had to walk out of the meetings to vent his anger in the hallway. He argued over every decision—it didn't even matter what it was. Every time they met, Deena thought it would be different. And every time she was wrong. Although she was desperate to collaborate, she was finally able to admit to herself that that wasn't what they were doing. Twenty thousand dollars later, they each had to pick new attorneys.

Collaboration is a great system for those who are able to collaborate. If you and your husband are at serious odds, it may not be for you.

The first step to getting the things you want out of life is this: Decide what you want.
—BEN STEIN

Q My husband went to one of the lawyers on my list to interview and rejected him. Can I hire him?

A If your husband has consulted with a lawyer, that same lawyer is not able to represent you. It's called a conflict of interest. In fact, if any members of the law firm represent your husband in any way (such as for business or real estate), you are not able to consult the firm. Hopefully you will be notified of this beforehand. In small towns this can became a problem because the lawyer may have an association with your husband either socially or through town issues. If you live in a small town, I advise looking for someone to represent you from a nearby town.

Keep in mind that no matter how cute and sexy a guy is, there's always some woman somewhere who's sick of him.

— CAROL HENRY

Q I met with a lawyer I really like and wanted to hire him on the spot but have been told not to do that. Do I trust my gut? How many lawyers should I interview and why?

A Remember that you are dealing in unfamiliar territory, so you should not go by your gut until you've gathered enough information. As a rule, I suggest you see three lawyers or mediators to make comparisons. Each will likely have a different view of your situation and move you in a slightly different direction. Although not likely, it's always possible that some may not be interested in your case after hearing the details.

On occasion a lawyer evaluates your financial situation and concludes you either don't have the money to pay or there isn't enough money at stake to make the case interesting. Suzy, a restaurant hostess, consulted a lawyer in her town who knew of her husband Carl's reputation as having questionable business ethics. He suspected that Carl would make everything into an issue, dragging the case on and on, and since he had a small practice, he declined to take Suzy as a client, in spite of the fact that he wanted to help her. To his credit, the lawyer was up-front with Suzy and recommended other lawyers for her to consult.

Marriage is really tough because
you have to deal with feelings . . . and lawyers.
—RICHARD PRYOR

QI understand that when I hire a lawyer I sign a retainer agreement. Can I negotiate any of the terms, and what should I be looking for?

ARetainer agreements outline the terms of your representation. I always advise my clients to take them home and read them carefully. Ask questions if you don't understand. This is a contract, and just like any contract, you have a right to negotiate it. Aside from naming the parties involved, the retainer should fully explain the services to be rendered and the fees to be charged. Take a look at the retainer agreement and discuss the following questions/issues:

- Do you receive a refund of the unused retainer fee if you decide to discontinue the case or change lawyers?
- How often will you be billed and how detailed will the bills be?
- Will the fees remain stable throughout your case? If not, how long before an increase will be made?
- All copies of correspondence, whether from your lawyer, his lawyer, or the court, are to be given to you.
- You must approve all crucial or sensitive correspondence on your case issued by your attorney. This prevents inaccuracies.

- You must be notified of any changes in billing in writing.
- Be clear who will represent you throughout the case. Large firms have many lawyers.
- Your lawyer should not place a lien on your property as a method of collecting fees.
- No payment will be made as a bonus on the basis of results.

This last point was important to one of my clients. Valerie's lawyer hired an accountant to evaluate her husband's business operations, and the accountant discovered that the total value of the operation was 25 percent higher than her husband claimed. Because her lawyer had insisted that an independent accountant be hired, Valerie became entitled to a larger sum of money. As a result, the lawyer claimed he was entitled to a financial bonus. I explained to my client this was unethical. According to the contract they'd signed, his fees were based on time spent only.

*The pure and simple truth is
rarely pure and never simple.*
— OSCAR WILDE

How Do I Hire a Lawyer?

Q A friend of mine just got divorced. She paid her lawyer a retainer but then wasn't billed until the very end. Is that the way it usually is handled?

A It should not be handled that way; your lawyer should be billing you monthly. This issue should be dealt with in your retainer agreement. Your bill should contain a breakdown of hours, including hours spent on conversations, letter writing, and meetings, and should identify the people your lawyer is communicating with. Lawyers charge in increments of tenths of an hour based on an hourly rate that is contained in your agreement (contract). If your lawyer charges $210 an hour, a three-minute phone conversation costs $21. The minutes add up quickly. As the client you should be tracking the time you take on the phone or in meetings with your lawyer. Make those minutes count. Be organized with your questions and don't spend your costly time complaining about your husband.

Q My lawyer never calls me back. I feel that my divorce isn't exciting or lucrative enough to keep her attention. I am frustrated and angry but don't want to antagonize her. I want her on my side. What should I say?

A This is a constant complaint; however, you must remember that while you are in a crisis and experience ups and downs during your difficult divorce process, this is business as usual for your lawyer. She probably doesn't feel the same urgency that you do. And of course you are not her only client, so it's often a matter of literal availability. If you are working with a lone practitioner, getting her on the phone at a moment's notice is always a problem because there is only one person—her—to deal with all client issues.

You should also be careful about how often you call. Don't be the girl who cried wolf! If you call for every little incident, your lawyer is guaranteed not to return your calls promptly. Try to deal with matters yourself; if it's a true emergency or an impossible situation, then make the call.

E-mail is another method of communication but should also be used with caution. With e-mail you have a record of exactly what you said.

To save time and money when communicating with your lawyer, make notes beforehand. Be prepared to get to the point promptly and efficiently. You will be billed for your lawyer's time, so use it wisely. Remember something important: You have employed your lawyer to assist you in the process, and you deserve her attention. If you've been a hostile client or a constant caller with unimportant complaints and questions, you could be the last to receive a return phone call. Lawyers are human, too.

How Do I Hire a Lawyer?

The relationship you cultivate with your legal counsel is a key ingredient in the success of your divorce. If you are intelligent and capable, you will gain the attention and respect of your counsel. This should be a partnership. Using him effectively requires following guidelines that I feel are necessary to repeat:

- Avoid the temptation to make your lawyer the savior who makes your decisions and tells you what to do. Remember this is your life and you will have to deal with it in the end.

- Be clear about what you feel your needs and wants are, but be careful to listen to what the lawyer thinks is reasonable and realistic. After all, you've hired her because she's a professional with experience and you want her to guide you (not lead you) through the turmoil.

- Be as efficient and timely with the materials your lawyer requests.

- Organize yourself and don't call all the time to rehash why your marriage failed or to complain about your husband's behavior. Doing this will cause you to rapidly lose your lawyer's attention and respect.

- At the same time, don't be afraid to be assertive and question your lawyer's advice. Your divorce is one

of the most serious business deals you will ever be
involved in.

Remember, your lawyer is knowledgeable about the
law, but *you* are the one knowledgeable about yourself and
your needs.

FOUR

WHAT HAPPENS IN THE COURTROOM?

Understanding the Before, During,
and After of a Divorce Trial

Don't expect to use the court system to help you express your anger, disgust, and frustration with your estranged husband. If you do, you will find little or no satisfaction. Court is not the place for vengeance. The court system won't even deal with who's to blame—that's not the purpose of going before a judge for a divorce settlement. If you enter the courtroom expecting to settle a score or figure out who is right and who is wrong, you'll be sorely disappointed—and a lot poorer in the process.

The objective of divorce court is to deal with tangibles such as money, children, and your postdivorce rights. The system is designed to resolve and dissolve the institution known as marriage, and it encourages the resolution in the form of an agreement between the two parties. The process begins with the filing of a motion to dissolve the marriage on specific grounds. At this point, a judge is assigned to the case. The judge is generally present to help resolve individual issues before a trial is required. In this chapter, we'll go over the most common questions women face as they're preparing to enter the courtroom and start the legalities of the divorce process.

Q Friends tell me that filing for divorce is a no-brainer. Should I do it myself or wait for my lawyer to do it?

A This answer will vary depending on the laws in your state. If you live in a state that doesn't require you to prove grounds for divorce and you don't anticipate a contentious or complicated divorce, you will have nothing but a straightforward form to fill out. If you feel comfortable doing so on your own, go ahead and file this form without hiring a lawyer. Your local courthouse will have the form for you to look over at home. Additionally, some states have lawyers in courthouses who can help you; some charge fees based on a sliding scale, and some provide their services free of charge (pro bono). Check with your courthouse. Or you can have your lawyer fill out the form for you.

Some women are more comfortable getting a professional to take care of this step, or they just can't bring
themselves to deal with the reality of the situation and
would prefer to pay someone to handle the messy details.
In the states that require more documentation to start
the divorce proceedings, or in divorces that will likely
be complicated and contentious, it may be best to hire
a lawyer from the very start and leave this to him. If
you're anticipating paying legal fees anyway, hiring your
lawyer to file this form will probably be a drop in the
bucket compared to your total legal fees—in terms of
your lawyer's time, this filing shouldn't even take an
hour. You may want to discuss the filing cost and possible
ramifications with your lawyer if you're unsure of which
path to select.

Q Can you give me a general idea of what the se-
quence of events will be during my divorce proceedings?

A One of the toughest parts of going through divorce is
the not knowing—not knowing what comes next, or
who the different players are in the drama, or even when to
expect the next stage of the process! Understanding the big
picture is so vital to your peace of mind during this emotionally draining time, and it's something that your lawyer

(even a good lawyer) may be too busy to take the time to explain to you. I've seen over and over again how understanding the general format and time frame of the divorce process helps to ease the tension and anxiety involved in the complex procedures. That's why clients often turn to a divorce coach like me to help them navigate the complex and intimidating process—and it's this information that I'll pass along to you in this book.

The most important thing to keep in mind is that divorces move on an established (and often slow) timetable. This can be particularly frustrating for women who enjoy planning and scheduling their lives. You have to give up a measure of control during this process! Be prepared for one hurry-up-and-wait episode after another: You rush to get your case into the system . . . and then you'll wait. And wait. If it's a contentious or complicated divorce, the wait can get even longer.

Here's a quick overview of each step in the divorce process. We'll explore each one in a bit more detail later in this chapter.

STEP 1: **The Complaint.** The plaintiff files papers with the court stating that the marriage is over and making basic claims and pleadings. Each state has its own format, but certain basic information is required:

- Residence(s) of you and your husband
- Date and place of marriage
- Names and birth dates of your children
- The reason(s) for your divorce
- List of claims, including requests for temporary maintenance, child support, custody terms, and asset division

STEP 2: **The Response.** Within a certain period of time (usually thirty to sixty days) the opposing spouse (the defendant) files an answer. The answer may be in agreement with or dispute the complaint.

STEP 3: **Pretrial Orders.** These are temporary orders filed with the court requesting that temporary arrangements be decided by the judge, including financial issues, custody, the prevention of the sale of assets, or orders for protection. For example, if your husband moves out and your children remain in the house with you, a judge may rule that your husband needs to pay a certain amount of child support and maintenance for the mortgage while the divorce proceedings are under way. These pretrial orders are binding and usually contain a term "without prejudice," meaning that these orders cannot automatically become part of the agreement.

STEP 4: **Discovery.** This is the process used to obtain information not voluntarily provided. Lawyers gather all the relevant papers about your marriage—including bank account statements, ownership papers (for real estate, retirement accounts, pension accounts, and trusts), loan applications, wills, and credit card statements—that detail how you and your husband live, how you earn your money, and what you might each reasonably expect to take away from the marriage. This information-gathering process and witnesses provide the material that will be used as the basis for the trial, should it get to that point. Discovery is exactly what it sounds like: discovering information that may or may not be easy to find, and may or may not be given voluntarily. It is mostly financial—asset and income and debt information—but can also encompass behavior, including issues like adultery and abuse.

STEP 5: **Depositions.** Out-of-court (usually but not always in one of the lawyers' offices) meetings between both spouses and attorneys, recorded in the presence of a court reporter and under oath, where issues and claims are questioned. Each spouse is questioned by the opposing lawyer about matters involved in the divorce, such as health issues, income, assets, and the documents gathered during the discovery process. During a deposition, other individuals can appear to give testimony. This is the place where both sides have an opportunity to assess the issues and problems and avoid surprises. It is here, too, that you can access your husband's case. This procedure forms the foundation for the negotiation of a written agreement; if not, a trial may be necessary.

STEP 6: **Trial.** If the spouses are unable to come to an agreement on the terms of the divorce after the discovery and deposition phases, your case will go to trial. I want to stress that very few divorce cases go to trial, but preparation for a possible trial is the focus of all the actions taken during the divorce process.

If a trial does occur, it also has several distinct stages:

- Each lawyer makes an opening statement and presents the issues involved.
- The plaintiff's lawyer presents his case, complete with documents or witnesses. The defendant is allowed to cross-examine the plaintiff and the plaintiff's witnesses.
- The defendant's lawyer presents evidence to counter the plaintiff's case, also complete with documents or witnesses. The plaintiff's lawyer is allowed to cross-examine the defendant's witnesses and the defendant.
- A rebuttal by the plaintiff: the opportunity to deny the defendant's material accusations or to discredit the witnesses or documents.

- Closing arguments: Each side summarizes the evidence.
- Judge's decision: Depending on the state, the judge may take several days, several weeks, or several months to make a decision.

Q Do all divorces get resolved with a trial?

A In most cases, no. The states have developed a program of rules that encourage an agreement, negotiated by the parties, as the appropriate method for resolution.

Q Under what circumstances might my divorce case go to trial?

A In general, disputes over finances and child custody are the main reasons for a trial to occur. And while trials are rare, when they occur they can be spectacularly messy, extremely prolonged, and very expensive for both parties. As one divorce lawyer I know tells his clients, "You can either put your kids through college or mine."

Divorces that do go to trial tend to get ugly, and Claire's was no exception. After many months of pretrial preparation, Claire's divorce went to trial in order to determine the value of her husband Frank's medical practice. The trial went on for several days; Frank was the plaintiff and presented his case first. His witnesses brought up personal and financial details about Claire and Frank's life together and attempted to present Claire as a detriment to her husband's position as the head of a prominent division of their local hospital. Frank also presented financial information about his private medical practice that made it seem less valuable than it really was, minimizing his total earnings and thus making him liable for less alimony support.

After several days, it was Claire's turn to present her side. Her attorney planned to talk about how Claire had put her own career as an advertising executive on hold while she was busy helping Frank build his practice; she had helped establish him in the medical community by generously entertaining in her home and by participating in many local charities. Claire was a fixture in their town and made the couple visible to important people.

Fortunately, we had discussed her relationship with the partners in her husband's medical practice. Would they be witnesses for her? Because of their ongoing relationship with her husband, probably not. However, two years before her divorce action, a former partner had been asked to leave in a very adversarial situation. Would the former partner be willing to establish the financials of the practice (which Claire maintained gave her husband a much higher income than he had reported)? The former partner agreed, and he testified at the trial to great effect. Ultimately, the judge realized how manipulative and dishonest Frank had been, and Claire was favored in his final decision.

The system is really set up to avoid having to go to trial, however, and divorces go to trial in a small percentage of cases. During the discovery and deposition processes, all parties should be looking for common ground and trying to find ways to resolve the situation outside the courtroom. Usually, both parties can come to an agreement before the last recourse of a trial. Trials are very expensive and anxiety producing, and there are no guarantees of the outcome. You'll find that judges advocate very strongly for a settlement rather than taking a case to trial. An agreement made through the efforts of both parties and their attorneys is nearly always more equitable.

But if your case does go to trial, you should know that there is no jury involved in divorce court—the decision is made by the judge alone. Just like any other trial, both sides can call witnesses, enter documents into evidence, and cross-examine the other party's witnesses. In the end, the judge renders the decision.

Even if a case goes to trial, it may not make it all the way to a judge's ruling. I have seen many cases in which the parties have halted the trial midway and signed an agreement instead.

I suggest you do whatever you can to avoid a trial. You do not want a judge, a disinterested third party, making decisions about your life. Additionally, it is extremely expensive to go to trial: The hours for preparation and for the trial itself are both very costly. At a trial, no one wins— except both attorneys.

<hr />

Any intelligent woman who reads
the marriage contract, and then goes into it,
deserves all the consequences.

—ISADORA DUNCAN

<hr />

Q When will I know whether my case will go to trial or not?

A When a divorce action becomes highly volatile and the two parties appear not to have agreement on any level, the lawyers will begin preparing the case for trial. This does not necessarily mean a trial will take place. Although most divorce cases are settled beforehand, trial preparation is necessary in case an agreement cannot be reached between the spouses.

Charles, a successful but cantankerous bankruptcy attorney, was used to taking charge of everyone and everything and thought he could take charge of his divorce. He dictated and corrected almost all the correspondence his lawyer issued and tried to negotiate the terms of the divorce agreement with his wife, Jada, via a barrage of e-mails. Charles had been domineering in their marriage, and he was continuing that pattern now. Every time he made an offer of one thing he threatened Jada that he would withhold something else—but the biggest problem occurred when he threatened to seek custody of their two children, ages three and five, based on the allegation that Jada was an alcoholic and unable to care for them. Jada was totally intimidated by his badgering, but she also worried that he might have a case should they go to court. Jada admitted to both me and her attorney that she'd had a problem with alcohol in the past. But she assured us that she had never put her children at risk and vowed that she would continue to do everything necessary to prevent a trial from taking place and possibly losing custody. Jada had attended treatment in an outpatient facility and was continuing to attend AA meetings on a regular basis, demonstrating to the courts that she was making an honest effort to overcome her problem. By the time the case was nearing trial, Jada was able to prove that she had been sober for more than twelve months, and Charles realized that the courts would look favorably on her efforts. He was forced to admit that he had no grounds for suing for full custody, and the trial did not take place. Jada was proactive, which was her best defense.

The bottom line is that you never know for certain whether a case is going to go to trial or whether it will be resolved outside the courtroom. All you can do is be as prepared as possible and arm yourself with the information and the facts to defend yourself should the worst occur.

Usually when people are sad, they don't do anything.
They just cry over their condition.
But when they get angry, they bring about a change.

—MALCOLM X

Q Is a judge necessary?

A It's not a choice: A judge is always assigned to your case, and he stays assigned to your case forever— unless, of course, he retires or is moved to another area of the court system. Not only is it not a choice whether to have a judge or not, it isn't your choice who your judge is. The judge's job is to help the lawyers facilitate an agreement between the opposing sides. Often the judge is called in before the trial to make decisions regarding support issues, asset rights, evaluation issues, and children's rights. If there is an impasse, the judge makes the final ruling.

Q My husband is completely unreasonable and we argue about every little thing. Do judges ever get fed up and make the final decision?

A Yes, sometimes this can happen. You don't want this to happen, but sometimes it's necessary. However, judges don't make decisions unless they are called to do so via a legal vehicle like a motion, a divorce complaint, or a contempt action (filed when someone has not followed a judge's order).

Barbara and Jonathan, both actors, had one of the most contentious divorces I have ever seen. When Barbara came to me, Jonathan was using his anger to hold up any responsible settlement. He was completely unreasonable, denying almost everything she requested. Every issue was brought via a motion before the judge for a decision. Finally the judge, with the help of his law clerk, drafted an agreement based on what he thought was fair and reasonable without knowing the necessary details and the background that the lawyers were familiar with. The couple was told that this document would become the final separation agreement for their divorce within ninety days. They were only allowed to make minor adjustments regarding the children but not the financial issues. This is rare and certainly not an ideal scenario.

Q **My lawyer keeps saying the judge will decide the matters my husband keeps refusing to deal with. Does this mean we will go to trial?**

A No. If you and your husband are unable to agree on issues that require immediate attention (such as temporary support, child visitation schedules, requests for net worth statements and counsel fees, among others) your judge will be called upon to intervene. It costs money to have a judge intervene because both sides have to submit a motion explaining the reasons why the issue cannot be resolved. Documentation is required as proof of an issue. The more documentation you have, the stronger your case will be to the judge.

Helene and her husband, Frank, spent three months going over budgets for her temporary support and child support. She wanted to be in control of her day-to-day and household expenses such as rent, gas, electricity, and telephone, so that she would see what it actually cost to run her household. She felt strongly that she needed to learn—and be in control of—all the financial matters she had ignored during their marriage. Frank refused to cooperate: He claimed she was irresponsible, paid bills late, was disorganized, and wouldn't keep track of the bills. He said her negligence would negatively impact his credit rating. After reading through all the documents, the judge granted Helene's request. The real reason for Frank's resistance was that he wanted to keep secret that he had been billing household expenses to his business.

Q**What does "grounds for divorce" mean?**

A"Grounds for divorce" refers to the reasons, in the legal documents, for the divorce. Most states are "no fault," meaning it isn't really necessary to prove anyone's at fault that the marriage is dissolving; the reason can be incompatibility or irreconcilable differences and does not require proof. In some states, however (New York State being one of them), the plaintiff is required to prove their grounds for divorce, such as cruel and inhuman treatment, abandonment, adultery, or imprisonment.

Q**What is a deposition?**

AA deposition or EBT (examination before trial) requires one party at a time to be questioned under oath before each other and both lawyers. This is usually held in one of the lawyers' offices. A deposition gives each party the right to hear testimony and seek documents pertaining to the issues. It gives both attorneys and their clients an overview of the finances, strengths and weaknesses of the case and of the witnesses involved before they go before the court. Depositions are used in all lawsuits.

Most clients are concerned and frightened by the very idea of a deposition, because in their mind they think a deposition means their case is definitely going to trial. I assure you this is not necessarily the case. A deposition is one of the key methods used to find out the specifics of the case so that a trial can be avoided in many instances.

One of the most common topics in a deposition is finances. In the deposition, you will be privy to your husband's earnings, income, asset pool, and the worth of his practice or business, if he owns one. And he will be privy to all this information about you. It's imperative that you are truthful and thorough—and that you keep a keen eye out for this same standard of truth in your husband's testimony.

Remember the marital biography you wrote when you first hired your lawyer? It will come in handy now—think of all that you know about his finances and be sure he's disclosing everything. In many divorces, this area is the source of much contention. See chapter 5 for a more thorough discussion of finances in divorce.

When two people decide to get a divorce,
it isn't a sign that they "don't understand"
one another, but a sign that they have,
at last, begun to.

—HELEN ROWLAND

Q What is an affidavit?

A An affidavit is a sworn statement of fact (or fact as you know it to be, to the best of your ability), made in writing, signed by you, and in some states must be witnessed by a legal official. It usually accompanies a motion that is presented to the judge, including requests for temporary support, visitation rights, or temporary custody, who will stay in the house, and who will pay the bills. The affidavit is a written version of a request verifying that what you are requesting be considered.

For example, if your lawyer was to file a motion for

temporary support, a written request would be presented to the judge along with a budget and explanation. An affidavit would accompany this document to confirm this as an official request from you.

Q My husband doesn't want a divorce and won't move out of the house. How do I get him out? What if he won't go?

A Unless you are being abused, there is nothing you can do legally. This is one of the most common questions I am asked by my clients, but unfortunately, getting your husband out of the house is not simple. Most women try to use reason and persuade their husband that they will both be happier if he leaves. The conversation often goes like this: "We have decided to get divorced and have agreed that I will stay in the house with our children. You are going to move out eventually, so in the interests of peace and trying to keep things amicable, I think it would work best if you move out in the next X months." Some women I know have asked for six months, while others have asked for two. It depends upon your own comfort level and what is reasonable given your relationship and situation.

If you do end up sharing the same space, be prepared for a lengthy and contentious battle. I have known lawyers who encourage the husband to dig his heels in and stay to the bitter end—sometimes simply to pressure the wife with his presence, thereby hoping to get her to move the divorce process more quickly. Sometimes it's a matter of money, and sometimes the husband just doesn't want to face the breakup of the marriage.

Sarah, the president of a company that goes to people's homes to help them organize, and her husband, John, were both ready to get out of their marriage. In fact, they had agreed on most aspects of their divorce. John, a chronic procrastinator, said he would look for an apartment, but he was dragging his heels and driving Sarah crazy. There was no question that they were jeopardizing the peace they had worked so hard to establish. As luck would have it, a mutual friend, who didn't know about their divorce, called Sarah to say she was moving out of state and wanted to know if they knew anyone who was looking for a three-bedroom apartment—just a mile away from their home. Sarah handed the phone to John, who went later that day to see the apartment. It was impossible for him to say no. It was lovely, it was close to his children, and it was reasonably priced. But the truth is, without that push, he was not motivated enough to leave. I have known several women who gritted their teeth and actually found their soon to be ex-husband a place to live.

Of course, sometimes taking action on the divorce itself gives both parties the peace of mind to wait on the decisions about their living situation. As soon as Jessie, a novelist, and her husband, Arnold, a salesman, made the decision to divorce, Jessie found that things were more clear-cut and that living with him was easier. On the other hand, many times it's simply impossible to remain under the same roof. Beth, a mother of three, caught her husband, Larry, viewing child pornography; she couldn't stand to have him in the house and needed him out immediately. Their judge ordered him out of the house, and there isn't a judge in the country who wouldn't do the same.

But if persuasion doesn't work and there are no clear-cut grounds for getting your husband out, be sure to keep your lawyer updated. Most courts won't force the husband (or wife, for that matter) to move out until there is either a separation agreement or a final divorce decree (depending on the state). And many people feel that it doesn't make sense to start dividing the family's financial assets so early in the game. This is one of the most difficult phases, but the truth is, unless your husband is abusive—physically or emotionally—he has as much right to stay in your home as you do. Certainly if things get out of hand, you can seek a restraining order and get him legally removed. The bottom line: Don't move out.

Q What should I do if I have been abused?

A If you have been physically abused, report it to the police immediately so they can bear witness to your injuries. If your husband is present and the abuse has just occurred, the police can issue an arrest on the spot. Next you must file an affidavit with the police department and follow through with the court system to get a restraining order from a judge. Your husband will be required to leave the household. Proving emotional abuse requires witnesses willing to file affidavits confirming the use of abusive language.

Do not dwell in the past, do not dream of the future, concentrate the mind on the present moment.
— THE BUDDHA

Q My husband won't move out and I can't stand it anymore. If I leave the house voluntarily can I get back in?

A Yes, you can move back in. Until otherwise decided, the house is still jointly owned. However, unless you have a written agreement with your husband that establishes your right to leave, some judges will view this decision as disrespectful of the laws that bind a marriage, especially if children are involved. If you do move out, you cannot take your children unless you can prove that your husband is abusive, either emotionally or physically. Also, unless legally agreed upon, you cannot use marital assets to finance your move.

Q **My husband moved out six months ago and most of his personal possessions are still in the house. He said he would come for them three months ago but didn't. Can I throw them away?**

A No. As frustrating as it is, and as good as it might feel to get his possessions out of your home for good, my advice to you is don't do it. He is still entitled to space in the household because you are still married. Hold back those impulses and get focused on what you are entitled to have. If you throw all his stuff out, you are not acting in good faith in the eyes of the law. It pays to be the good guy. If you do throw his stuff out, your husband will surely bring this up with the judge and paint you as vindictive.

Any change, even a change for the better,
is always accompanied by
drawbacks and discomforts.
—ARNOLD BENNETT

Q **When are we legally separated?**

A This varies hugely from state to state. As a rule, you are legally separated when a separation agreement containing all the issues governing your divorce is signed by both of you and filed with the court. You also need to have been living separately for a period of time. In New York, Hawaii, and Utah, the separation agreement becomes a formal divorce decree if there are no fault issues involved. However, each state requires a period of time to pass before the separation agreement is combined with the divorce decree.

*The difference between a divorce and
a legal separation is that a legal separation gives
a husband time to hide his money.*

—JOHNNY CARSON

Q What's the difference between a separation agreement and a divorce decree? What is contained in a separation agreement?

A A separation agreement is, in many ways, an interim document that is filed on the way to a divorce decree. In the end, a separation agreement will be incorporated into the final decree for divorce. The agreement will typically address all aspects of the separation:

- The right to reside separate and apart
- The right to separate ownership of property
- Mutual release of claims of estates (renouncing all rights in the property of the other)
- Property settlement payments in accordance with equitable distribution laws, including transfer of

stocks, bonds, bank accounts, cash, pension funds, jewelry, automobiles, art, business interests, and the transfer of title on real estate the wife (or husband) will own

- Maintenance (alimony): This clause deals with the amount of support, the length of time it will be received, and how the payments will come, usually on a monthly basis.

- Child support issues and emancipation: This is the monthly support amount for the day-to-day expenses incurred while the children live in the primary household. This section includes the noncustodial parent's responsibilities for any add-on expenses including school tuition, nonreimbursed medical expenses, special lessons, and tutoring. The higher the income of the noncustodial parent, the more expenses he or she will pay.

- Custody and visitation rights

- Counsel fees

- Life insurance for the obligation of the parents for child support

- Debt and credit card responsibilities

*The divorced person is like a man with
a black patch over one eye: He looks rather dashing
but the fact is that he has been through
a maiming experience.*

—JO COUDERT

Q What is a prenuptial agreement and how secure is it?

A A prenuptial or marital agreement is usually drawn up prior to the marriage (although sometimes it is created after the marriage and then is known as a postnuptial). A prenuptial agreement (or prenup) is an agreement that outlines the rights and financial obligations due if a divorce should occur. Prenups are most often used for people who have acquired great wealth prior to their marriage as a way to protect their finances. It's also appropriate to use one to protect your estate for your children if a remarriage occurs.

The process usually requires both parties to exchange net worth statements (a breakdown of all they own individually and its value) as well as their income and earnings.

Supporting documents include brokerage statements, bank statements, deeds to real property, partnership positions, pensions, and IRA plans. Both parties must retain their own lawyers to confirm their understanding and the accuracy and legality of the document before signing the agreement. When a couple has signed a prenuptial agreement and those agreements are truthful and complete, it is rare for the court to set the agreement aside unless fraud due to nondisclosure or false disclosure can be proved.

Q **When should I change my will?**

A You can change your will anytime you wish. However, while you are still married and the divorce is pending, you can execute a will that provides your estranged husband with the minimum required spousal share of your estate. At the time you do this, be sure to stipulate that no part of your estate shall pass to him upon the finalization of the divorce decree.

Q **I originally filed for divorce. My husband is insisting that we change it so that we are on record as filing jointly. Does it matter who files?**

A In general, it makes little difference. The person who files first is the plaintiff and the other is the defendant.

What Happens in the Courtroom?

If you end up in court, it's better to be the defendant because the plaintiff makes the first move, allowing you to
have an overview of his strategy.

Experience is the name everyone gives
to their mistakes.

—OSCAR WILDE

Q How easy is it to get a divorce in a no-fault state?

A Unfortunately, not easy. Several years ago I had a client
who came with just this question. Janet had been un-
happily married for fifteen years to Steven, a very successful
financier. They lived in a large house in the suburbs outside
of New York City with all the trappings of a rich lifestyle,
including luxury cars, household help, lavish vacations,
and two accomplished children. On the outside it looked
picture perfect, but Janet claimed there was no relationship at its heart. Steven was too busy with his job and was
never home. When he put in a rare appearance, he criticized
everything Janet did: how she looked, how she cooked, and

what she allowed the children to do. Most of the time he yelled at her and belittled her in front of the children. When they appeared at social events, which was quite often due to his business, he dictated what she should wear and what she should say. For Janet, it was like living in a prison. She had no money available to her and had to request permission to make major purchases for the house and the children. At the beginning of each month he deposited a limited "allowance" for her personal needs, and she was required to keep her expenses within that amount. He paid all the bills and signed her name to the tax returns so that she had no knowledge of their finances. According to Janet, Steven was perfectly content and had no intention of divorcing her. He felt it was beneficial for the children to have two parents at home and that Janet wasn't deprived because he gave her ample money to take care of her needs. On her own she'd never make it. She hadn't worked in years and had no skills. He said he'd fight for custody of the children.

I had to explain to Janet that she needed to prove grounds to divorce him in New York State. In almost any other state a spouse can quit a marriage without a reason prescribed by law. New York State does not grant a divorce for incompatibility or irreconcilable differences. There are four grounds for fault in New York. (In other words, the state requires one spouse to be at fault and the other has to prove it.) The legal grounds are:

- Cruel and inhuman treatment. The treatment must be proven to have such a serious effect on the physical or mental health of the spouse that it would not be safe to continue the marriage.
- Abandonment. This claim comes into play if your spouse has left without your consent and without justification for one or more years.
- Imprisonment for three or more years
- Adultery, which is not uncommon but not necessarily a simple matter to prove unless you have a witness and documentation

Unfortunately for Janet, unless her husband cooperated with a divorce, her efforts to prove cruel and inhuman treatment were unlikely to be accepted by the court.

New York and a few other no-fault states are still laboring under old-fashioned methods, and although there have been rumors of change, nothing has happened. There are countless stories of husbands and wives who are trapped in dead marriages, and to my knowledge Janet is still one of them.

Another incident I encountered involved a woman named Terri. She described her life the same way Janet did, except that Terri's husband, Jack, told her he would grant a divorce if she would give up some of her financial rights. Otherwise, he said, he was perfectly content to remain married. I suggested Terri find out what rights he was referring to; in other words, in what way did his proposal differ from what the equitable distribution laws would entitle her to. In the end Terri was granted her divorce after she gave up her rights to money due her from the business he had. To Terri, her freedom was more important than the money.

Q Is there any way to obtain a divorce in a no-fault state without using fault grounds?

A Yes, all you need to do is have a separation agreement prepared by your attorneys that outlines the financial arrangements and the items we've listed in our discussion on what a separation agreement contains (see page 105). This document will allow the two parties to live separately and must be filed with clerk of the county the couple resides in. One year from the date of its filing either spouse may sue the other for a no-fault divorce, provided all the provisions of the agreement have been lived up to.

Q Can I use my maiden name after I'm divorced?

A This is a simple issue you can resolve without much effort and without the consent of your ex. It's your choice. All you have to do is have your divorce decree stipulate that you will once again become legally known by your maiden name. The banks, credit card companies, and other institutions that hold stock certificates or any legal documents you wish to change your name on will request a copy of this stipulation, which will be filed with the courts.

FIVE

WHAT DO I DO
ABOUT MONEY?

Learning How to Protect What's Yours and
Get What You Deserve

Regrettably, money is an issue that many women choose not to deal with during the course of their marriage. But during a divorce, understanding your finances is the most important piece of knowledge you need.

A good marriage is a partnership. How money is handled and how financial decisions are arrived at is an indication of the mutual trust and respect that underlies your relationship. It you are ignorant about your own financial picture, coming up with a monthly budget becomes a matter of guesswork—and unfortunately divorce is a very costly time to learn about it.

Even today, in the twenty-first century, it's amazing

to me how many married women are financially illiterate. Many of my clients either know nothing or too little about their family finances; they may know their husband's salary and bonus but don't know anything about the monthly expenditures for the family, pension plan, mortgage, health insurance, what debts they have, or how much is in their savings accounts. Too many women give up their voice when money is the issue, and for too many men it's a way of controlling the household. The law considers your marriage an economic partnership and will divide the finances in a divorce the way a business partnership divides its assets.

Here are a few suggestions concerning money issues. If you are in the midst of your divorce and realize that you haven't yet implemented many of the plans suggested here, don't worry: It's never too late.

- You should have a joint checking account, out of which you pay at least some of the monthly bills.
- There should be joint decisions on major expenditures.
- Tax return information should be available to and shared between both partners.
- In general you should see and keep records on bank accounts, brokerage accounts, insurance policies, wills, and credit cards.

What Do I Do About Money?

The biggest mistake is to remain ignorant about your finances and not discuss them with your spouse. Knowing about your money and making decisions are part of the partnership known as modern marriage.

When you are finally divorced, you will be in charge of your own finances, and how wisely you handle them will help determine your lifestyle. It can be a difficult time to reestablish yourself and adapt to a change in your lifestyle, but with this change comes independence as a reward.

Courage is being scared to death—
but saddling up anyway.
—JOHN WAYNE

Q **What is an asset property and how is it divided upon divorce?**

A An asset property refers to anything in the marriage that is held jointly—real estate, stocks, bonds, business interests, pensions, bank accounts, jewelry, furs, automobiles, furniture, antiques, and art objects. The time frame for acquisition begins at the start of your marriage and ends on the date the petition for divorce is officially filed with the court. In some states the values are set as of the date of the divorce. The fact that only your husband's name is on the deed to your house or the bank account does not mean it belongs solely to him. In today's world, title does not matter.

Q What is equitable distribution?

A Most states divide property based on equitable distribution. That means that your assets are divided based on what is determined to be equitable or fair, rather than equal. The longer the marriage, the greater your chances that an equitable division will also be an equal division.

Until recently, when states adopted equitable distribution rules, property ownership was based on the name the property was titled to and therefore the person with the title maintained ownership after the divorce. Matrimonial law primarily focuses on property division, and while specific laws vary from state to state, the law generally considers the following factors when determining equitable division of the property:

- Duration of the marriage
- Age and health of the parties

- Income of both parties prior to the marriage and at the time the divorce action began
- Contributions of each to the marriage whether as the earner or homemaker
- Presumed financial situation of both after the divorce
- Minor children involved
- Any wasteful dissipation of the marital assets

If you can clearly prove that your spouse has hidden assets; kept information from you; dissipated assets on paramours, gambling, or alcohol; or failed to support the family, you, as the innocent spouse, may be awarded a larger percentage of the financial pool. The general rule of thumb is the shorter the marriage, the more it matters who brought or contributed assets during the marriage. In a longer marriage matters of fault can determine that one party receive a larger share of the assets than the other.

Q A recently divorced friend always uses the word "maintenance" when referring to what I call "alimony." I am confused: What does "maintenance" mean in reference to divorce?

A "Maintenance" is the more modern word for the more old-fashioned "alimony." If you don't work outside the home, or if you make much less money than your husband, maintenance is the temporary support provided for you while you regain your independence. The amount and length of the monthly payment is determined by a number of factors, including your husband's salary, your age, health, length of marriage, asset pool, lifestyle, and your future earning potential.

Q Do I get a higher maintenance based on the length of my marriage?

A In the eyes of the law, marriage is considered a joint partnership. The longer you are married, the more time you have participated in the joint partnership and therefore the greater your financial rights. In determining your assets, the law looks at real estate, cash on hand, your husband's income, and your current income or ability to work (including age, health, and past employment) and subtracts the debts incurred.

Kate, age twenty-eight, had been married for five years and had a one-year-old child. She stopped working as a secretary when Mary was born. When they divorced, her husband Ken agreed to three years of maintenance to help Kate get back on her feet and child support until Mary graduated from college. This put Kate in the position to spend two years focusing on her daughter until she could attend preschool, at which time Kate would look for work.

What Do I Do About Money?

Jane, forty-two, came to me after being married for fifteen years. She had a freelance job writing a column for a local newspaper, which netted a small income that was used by the family as extra cash. She and Frank, her husband, lived above their means (he regularly dipped into his trust fund), and there was no question she would have to return to work after the divorce. However, Jane had multiple sclerosis, which flared up when she was put in a stressful work environment. We knew if this became a real issue in her divorce she would need the opinion of a doctor to verify the problem. We discussed Jane's options. Could she take on more freelance work at home? Could she depend on her large family for help if medical problems occurred? Were they close enough to be able to help out in a time of need? Could the two pieces of real estate the couple owned be sold to generate enough money to give her a cushion to draw interest from?

Through mediation, Jane and Frank were able to come to terms. They agreed that she would receive eight years of maintenance and that she and their daughter would move close to her family, where living expenses were lower and their daughter would have the advantages of a close family, good schools, and affordable housing. The only real problem was visitation, because living in another state meant Frank wouldn't have easy access to their daughter. As a result a schedule was developed that allowed him to have his daughter for two full months in the summer, the full

Christmas holiday every other year, and during her other vacations (so as not to upset her school schedule).

❧❧❧

What a holler would ensue if people had to pay the minister as much to marry them as they have to pay a lawyer to get them a divorce.

—CLAIRE TREVOR

❧❧❧

Q Are maintenance payments taxable?

A The IRS considers maintenance payments to be salary, which is therefore taxable. The payer receives a deduction for the payments on his or her tax return.

Q Is child support taxable?

A Child support is not viewed as income to the custodial parent, therefore it is not taxable. Child supports ends upon the emancipation of the child (which can be at age eighteen, twenty-one, or twenty-three, depending on the state), or upon the marriage or death of the child. Life insurance provides for the child if the supporting parent dies before emancipation.

Q Is maintenance determined by lifestyle?

A No. And yes. This is a myth if you are living beyond your means. This form of temporary support is a financial arrangement for the sole purpose of allowing the nonearner to reorganize her life and find a way to earn a living for the purpose of making her independent. Sometimes people go back to school to establish a new career.

Maintenance, whether determined by the judge or the lawyers, is based upon a realistic household budget determined by the money actually available. Often the lifestyle you lived together was financed by living beyond your means by incurring debt or accepting money from family members.

Divorce is the time of reckoning. I warn most of my clients that their lifestyles will change. This is the time you'll have to learn to live on a budget and stick to it.

Q I am thinking of accepting a higher paying job with a great firm but am worried that it will

decrease my maintenance payments. Should I accept
the job?

A Absolutely yes! While you will most likely lose all or
some of your financial support if an opportunity comes
your way, by all means take it. Why put yourself in a position of dependence, particularly since most maintenance
awards are temporary? Your future is what you should be
concerned about.

Q How has equitable distribution become an advantage for women?

A Equitable distribution was conceived with the idea that
marriage is an economic partnership based on not only
financial contributions but also on the unreimbursed services contributed to the partnership, such as homemaking,
child care, and emotional and moral support.

Q I am a stay-at-home mom. My husband gives me
what he calls my "allowance" and requires me to
show him how I spend it. How will this impact my
divorce?

A This appears to be a marriage where control rather
than equality exists. It's probably a sign of deeper
problems: This situation, which is unfortunately more

common than you would think, indicates that there is little trust or sharing when it comes to the family finances. Money is a control factor in many marriages and one of the most important issues in a divorce. As soon as Barbara told me that she had a set amount of money (sometimes referred to by both spouses as the "monthly allowance") allotted to her to deal with the day-to-day expenses, I knew what was in store. In many of these situations the wife has no knowledge about the family finances. Jennifer, a nurse, told me that her salary paid for her personal expenses plus child care. When Russ, her husband, determined that they didn't need a new couch, or that their daughter didn't need to go to a certain camp, she would pay for those expenses out of her earnings. Whenever she spent "his" money on items considered outside the daily household expenses, she was required to present the bills to him. These items might be gifts to friends or businesspeople, entertainment expenses, etc. When she asked questions concerning the family's overall money situation, Russ told her that she wouldn't understand and that he was in charge. Jennifer signed the tax returns and knew what Russ earned but didn't understand the family finances and was too intimidated to ask questions.

For complicated reasons many women are afraid to deal with money issues and allow their husbands to bully them. In Jennifer's case I suggested she accumulate copies of the bills as they arrived at the house and receipts for all the items she herself paid for. We were developing a paper trail, both to establish her contributions and to establish a realistic understanding of the financial situation. Were they living beyond their means? Was her husband determined to maintain control? Because of Jennifer's lack of financial knowledge the divorce process became more complicated and more costly since much of her lawyer's time was spent obtaining financial documents. I always like to remind my clients that knowledge is power.

If your husband gives you a meager amount of money, this reflects on his personality but not on the ultimate amount of support you may get. It will help you show the court how controlling he is.

Q Over the course of our marriage my husband often gave me gifts of jewelry. Are they included in our list of assets to divide?

A Expensive jewelry (worth a thousand dollars and up) received from your husband during your marriage is considered a marital asset and therefore up for evaluation if your husband requests it. The value would need to be set by a professional jewelry appraiser at fair market value rather than what was paid for the item. On the other hand, if you received gifts from family members or friends, they belong to you, not to the marital partnership. However, this, too, varies from state to state. In some states jewelry is counted as an asset no matter where it came from and is subject to equitable distribution; but where it came from can affect who retains it.

Janine's husband, Robert, had given her gifts of jewelry for every holiday, birthday, and anniversary both before and during their marriage. He insisted that his gifts totaled more than $150,000, which he wanted to have deducted from her asset payout. First they had to distinguish the "before" and "during" gifts. Gifts received before their marriage were not considered marital property. I advised Janine to get an appraisal to see if Robert's valuation was accurate, and guess what? It wasn't. His gifts were actually valued at $40,000. Originally, Janine thought she'd sell the jewelry and take the money; however, there was no guarantee that the sale at auction would bring her $40,000. In the end she kept the items, but they were credited to her asset payout.

Q I'm worried that once I file for divorce, my husband will seize some of our joint assets and claim them as his own. How can I protect the assets we have once we file for divorce?

A If you are married to someone who you suspect will take the assets you've acquired during the marriage, the court can protect you by issuing a restraining order. This order prevents the transfer or sale of marital assets, including cash, bank accounts, stocks, and real estate, prior to the valuation and division of the property.

Sally, a computer expert who earned her living developing software, could trace almost everything on the computer. She discovered that $25,000 had been withdrawn from the family savings account at the same time her husband, Joshua, a magazine editor, told her he wanted a divorce. In fact, there seemed to have been several large withdrawals over the past couple of months. She immediately tapped into his e-mail to see if she could trace where the money might have gone. She discovered, much to her dismay, correspondence with a woman about a trip to Europe for the following month. Sally then went to their checking account to see if there were any withdrawals that would tell her more. There were no checks out of the ordinary. The $25,000 seemed to have disappeared.

She came to me wanting to know what she could do about her discoveries. I suggested that she find a lawyer right away who could proceed with the action to prevent further dissipation of their marital funds. If Joshua had squandered assets shortly before the divorce filing, he set himself up for the court to question his honesty. This could only be done if she retained a lawyer and began divorce proceedings. It was decision time.

QI am concerned about health insurance: I am insured through my employer, and according to the laws in my state, I have to keep my husband on until one of us gets remarried. I am afraid that he won't reimburse me for his portion of the premium and won't pay his own bills on time. What can I do?

A Laws vary hugely from state to state, but the federal government requires that the uninsured spouse be covered for up to three years after the divorce is finalized. For example, New York and California law requires your husband to be eligible to continue his health insurance through a COBRA plan for three years, which means he will have a separate policy and you don't have to worry. In Massachusetts, on the other hand, the law requires that both parties can elect to stay on the same insurance until remarriage or death. Be very clear about the laws in your state. If you have to keep your husband on your policy, be sure to have something written into the agreement saying that he has to pay his premiums, co-pays, and out-of-pocket expenses on time and what the clear consequences are if he doesn't. For example, think baseball: Three strikes and you're out. In my experience, most judges will penalize when nonpayment becomes a pattern.

Q I haven't worked since before I got married forty years ago and I can't see joining the workforce now. Can I get lifetime support?

A "Lifetime support" (his lifetime, not yours) is a recent concept. Women who have been in a marriage for twenty or more years, are over fifty, and have little or no work history have the potential to receive lifetime support. There are several other factors that have to be considered: the size of the asset pool, the couple's lifestyle, the wife's contribution to that lifestyle, health issues, and the future earning capacity of her husband. This issue, too, varies from state to state; in my experience, after a motion is filed requesting it, the judge will make the decision.

Julie, a stay-at-home-mom who had been a nurse prior to her marriage, was awarded lifetime support when her divorce went to trial. Her husband, James, owned his own business and refused to recognize that her lifestyle would be critically altered due to her limited earning power; more important, his future earnings would continue to be sizable. The assets she received in her divorce wouldn't generate enough additional income to support her equitably.

Wanda was a former fashion model. At age thirty-nine, after having three children (now ranging in age from seven to twelve), she was still very beautiful but no longer had the figure the business required. Wanda had a divorced friend who received an award of lifetime support and she thought she too would be entitled to the same. What Wanda didn't factor in was that her friend was fifty-four and hadn't worked in more than twenty-five years. Also, although Wanda's husband was a very successful broker who earned substantial money, saving was not his style. This meant the asset pool was not adequate to sustain Wanda after the divorce. As far as the legal system was concerned Wanda was still young and capable of returning to the workforce. Her children were no longer babies and didn't require her to stay at home. Besides, she would receive child support to meet their needs. The lawyers structured an agreement that entitled her to several years of temporary support plus half the assets and a share in her husband's retirement fund, giving her adequate time to decide what she was going to do. In the end Wanda went back to school and became an interior designer.

Q My husband is not working right now but he got a very good buyout from his last job. Most of this money is invested and we are living off the investments. Is this considered income?

A This is considered his income and the money that provides your day-to-day way of life. It would not be treated any differently than a salary.

Q My husband and I have been supporting my elderly parents for our entire marriage. My husband makes about eight times what I make and I cannot afford to support them. What will happen upon our divorce?

A If your husband has been that generous during your marriage, with luck he will continue. However, he has no legal obligation to do so. You'll have to go it alone unless your husband wants to take care of them. His financial responsibilities are to you and any underage children only.

Q My husband is not the most accountable guy. I am afraid he won't live up to his agreements and that I will have to take him back to court. I hate the thought of spending even more money. Will we have to split the cost of going back to court?

A Generally yes, but sometimes no. The best advice I give my clients is to be sure to put a stipulation (a clause that defines the terms of responsibilities) in their final divorce agreement that covers responsibility of legal fees. The clause should read something like this: "If you are required to return to court to enforce the terms of the agreement, the opposing side will be responsible for all legal fees." Lawyer's fees are expensive and tend to increase over time. This kind of stipulation is a must if you have a husband who has been irresponsible or vindictive.

Jane had this problem with her husband, Daniel, who routinely paid child support and the add-on children's expenses (i.e., school tuition, medical expenses) several months late. Luckily her separation agreement contained this kind of stipulation, and when she took Daniel to court, he was forced to pay both his own and her legal fees. It taught him an expensive lesson. In some states, if one side disobeys a court order, the court can order the noncompliant spouse to pay all legal fees.

Q **My lawyer asked me to fill in some forms in reference to our taxes. My husband does the taxes, and I am ashamed to say I don't know what anything is. Where can I find this information?**

A It's a good idea to get and keep copies of your tax returns, especially if you are contemplating a divorce. This is an important step in establishing knowledge about your financial position. Ask questions when you sign any tax forms; signing them makes you just as responsible for the tax return as your husband.

Sometimes asking questions of an accountant is easier than asking your husband, who may feel threatened by your interest if you haven't been previously involved. If you are not used to reading tax returns, I suggest you focus only on the first two pages of the 1040 form, which will give you a quick overview of the finances without getting into the more complicated sections (which can make almost anyone's head spin). These pages give the gross income earned for the year, interest earned, other income different from salary, losses, tax paid during the year, how much is owed in taxes for the present year, and the net income for the year.

Once you have started the process, if you are reluctant to request the tax returns from your husband, have your lawyer request them for you. Remember that the point of divorce negotiation is trading certain assets for others and trying to end up with enough to continue your life.

Q We are still legally married but separated. Should we file taxes jointly or separately for this year?

A There is no right answer. You can choose to file a joint return with your husband or file a married-but-separate return. The option that creates the least liability for you or the biggest refund is the way to go.

When Kathy came to see me, her husband, William, owed back taxes, and she was concerned about his reporting methods. She had a job as a teacher and her taxes were deducted directly from her paycheck. William had his own business and took liberties with his deductions, and she suspected he often received cash that he didn't report. She chose to file married-but-separate taxes.

What Do I Do About Money?

Q What do I think about when putting a monthly budget together other than the obvious expenses like mortgages and utilities?

A One of the first things your lawyer or mediator will do is to give you a form to fill out known as a "net worth statement." I like to begin with the monthly budget. The form covers the general categories of housing, utilities, food, clothing (including clothing allowances for children), laundry, insurance, household maintenance, cars, children's expenses (including birthday parties and birthday presents), and personal and recreational costs. Focusing on this information will help you get a realistic grasp of your coming financial needs. The following are items people tend to forget to account for: property taxes, water and sewage costs, cleaning expenses, appliance repairs and maintenance, pocket money, dues and memberships, car repair expenses, haircuts, beauty supplies, dining out, life insurance costs, and Internet expenses.

Q I get the impression that my divorce would go a lot smoother and swifter if I gave my husband a larger share of our joint retirement funds accumulated over the course of our marriage. We're both pretty young and have time to earn more money—what's the harm in bending on this one issue?

135

A I would warn against doing this. You must realize that you are part of a partnership and entitled to the finances accumulated during that partnership. You should be looking at your future and preparing for it rather than buying your way out of the marriage. Too often women get anxious about the divorce procedure and are willing to give up anything to avoid emotional turmoil. This is not smart.

Q My husband and I have agreed that I will stay in the house with our kids. Should I try to buy him out right away or stretch it out until the kids graduate?

A It really depends upon your earning power and the needs of your children, yourself, and your ex-husband. Britt and her husband, Frank, were both high school teachers. They owned a two-family home and rented out one of the units. When they decided to get a divorce, Frank wanted to kick out the tenants and live downstairs while Britt and the children stayed upstairs. Although she entertained this crazy notion (against my advice), she eventually rejected it. Frank was furious and insisted they sell their house. That, too, was unrealistic. They eventually agreed that she would buy Frank out, giving him 25 percent upon signing their divorce agreement and the rest when their eight-year-old son graduated from high school. This is a very common scenario.

Q When my husband and I got married I had owned
my house for ten years. He moved in and built
an addition on the house. He is now claiming that he
should be reimbursed for his time and the expenses,
which we shared. Is this fair?

A It depends. After her marriage to John, Carrie, a pot-
ter, decided to enlarge her house, in part because John
was a builder. Although Carrie had no intention of selling
her house, John insisted it be appraised for the divorce
settlement. According to the real estate appraiser, John's
contribution raised the value of the house by 20 percent.
In this case John was entitled to money for his efforts.

If either the husband or wife is a builder or simply good
with a hammer and contributes to the improvement of the
house—financially, as a supervisor, or as a coordinator—
they would have a fair claim for reimbursement.

Q My husband has an expense account. How does
this factor into his income and net worth?

A Expense accounts play a part in establishing income.
Claudia had been married for thirty-four years when she
came to me to help determine what her husband was earning
and what kind of maintenance she was entitled to. By com-
paring their monthly expenses with his reported income,
we discovered that they were leading a lifestyle way beyond

their income. John owned his own construction business and had a hefty expense account. It became apparent that he was using the expense account to pay some of their living expenses, including car leases, restaurants, and travel, but reported them as business expenses, in order to save on taxes. In the end his expense account was factored into determining his income and therefore Claudia's support order.

Q My husband had a pension plan before we married. I say I am entitled to some but not all of it since he had it prior to our marriage. He says no. Who is correct?

A You are. Christina and her husband, Herb, an engineer, had been married for seven years when she came to see me. Herb's pension plan had started five years before their marriage and he continued to contribute to it during the seven years of their marriage. Since the law looks at marriage as a partnership, Christina had some rights to the funds that had accumulated in Herb's pension plan during the time of their marriage. The courts awarded her 25 percent of the value at the time of the divorce, which seemed fair to all. In this case, the standard fifty-fifty share distribution would not have given credit to Herb's earlier contributions. The exception to this might occur when there has been a marriage of long standing; the fact that some was premarital might not matter at all.

All marriages are happy. It's the living together
afterward that causes all the trouble.
— RAYMOND HULL

Q **What is a forensic accountant and what is his role in a divorce?**

A Forensic accountants are expert witnesses who put fair market dollar evaluations on businesses, professional assets, art collections, or other assets factored into a divorce settlement. Susan, a hair stylist, was in the midst of divorcing her husband, Roger, who owned a restaurant with three partners. This business was the primary source of their family's income. The judge appointed a forensic accountant to determine the fair market value of Roger's ownership, which was part of their joint assets.

Forensic accountants examine many complicated financial details to determine the dollar value of business and other assets, and in Susan's case the accountant helped her understand how to properly value her husband's business, which was largely a cash enterprise. The accountant looked at many factors, including the capital investment her husband (and therefore also Susan) had put in: ownership percentage, corporate tax returns, profit and loss statements, payroll records, expense accounts, the lease on the restaurant, future earnings projections, equipment value, cash on hand, outstanding credit cards, pension plans, restaurant provisions on hand and their value, future orders, and outstanding bills in order to value Roger's ownership.

In simple terms, Susan was being bought out of her share of the business partnership she (by virtue of marriage) and her husband owned. Since the restaurant existed several years before the marriage, Susan's share of Roger's part would be less then 50 percent. I told her that if she had made a substantial contribution to the business, her percentage could be open to determination. Susan had supervised the redesign of the restaurant about two years before the divorce action, which we believed had contributed to the total value of the business.

In the end the judge awarded her 35 percent of the value of her husband's share in the partnership, a figure that neither Susan nor her husband was totally pleased with, but one that both of them had to live with. When a judge makes the determination, it's based on how he sees the value, which may or may not be accurate. Again, it's always better to come to an agreement together than let a judge decide for you.

Among the many complicated business documents and details explored by the forensic accountants are:

- Corporate tax returns
- Profit, loss, and balance sheets
- Profit-sharing plans
- Employment records
- Payroll records
- Expense account details
- An overview of the competition and its impact on a family's business
- Any potential sale, including any offers for the business now or in the past
- The lease on the property
- The value of any equipment

Q How long will it take to be legally divorced? How much will it cost?

A There isn't a person who walks into my office who doesn't ask these questions, but I am sorry to say I cannot answer them with any accuracy. The time and money will depend on how complex the finances are and whether the divorce becomes a battleground. Costs depend on the hourly rate of the lawyer (ranging from two hundred to seven hundred dollars) but can be greatly impacted (and reduced) by how organized you are about what you want and need and how much you do for yourself, including gathering information and drawing up budgets.

The shortest time I have ever seen for a divorce involved a short-lived marriage with no children and no claims made against each other. It still took a year because of all the papers that have to be filed and the endless red tape of the legal process. However, if you are really in agreement and live in a no-fault state, your divorce can be heard as quickly as your agreement is committed to paper and signed.

The longest divorce I ever consulted on took ten years to resolve, because the couple fought about everything— literally everything (except, of course, how rich their lawyers were becoming).

If you want a quick divorce I suggest you pick your battles. Develop a strategy and focus. You have no control over the other person; all you can control is yourself. On the other hand, if your husband is stalling or angry, he may be determined to make the process difficult.

If you have your own money you will probably be responsible for paying your own fees; however, if your husband purposely exacerbates the situation, the court may make him pay your fees as well as his own.

Delilah's husband, Tony, was incredibly plodding. Every decision he made took forever. He either had to research every detail endlessly or took no action. During their divorce, Tony was, to Delilah's thinking, completely

unreasonable in the issues he insisted be examined, and
almost everything he was requested to do took a judge's
order to get done. He delayed forwarding financial information needed to evaluate the assets, didn't respond to
requests for information made by her lawyer, refused to pay
doctor's bills, was consistently late with child support and
school tuition, and generally dragged out the entire procedure. This took additional time and money and produced
overwhelmingly large legal fees. The judge saw Tony's
behavior as a deliberate way to deplete their finances and
ordered Tony to pay 75 percent of Delilah's legal fees.

Q I don't work and have no income of my own. How
do I pay for a lawyer? Why doesn't it just come
out of our joint bank account?

A Generally speaking, stay-at-home moms don't have
access to much other than checking accounts, which
are used for day-to-day expenses and don't contain the
five thousand to ten thousand dollars or more needed
for a retainer fee. This is a very difficult issue for women
who don't work outside the home. The best advice I can
offer you is to talk with your lawyer and discuss payment
options. Try to borrow the retainer from your family or
friends. If necessary, you can try to obtain a cash advance
against your credit cards, but make that the last alternative.
In most cases, you will be reimbursed for your expenses in

the financial settlement. Most lawyers will bill monthly but some may understand that they won't be paid until things are settled.

Q I am buying my husband out of our house. We bought it, in part, with money he put in from savings acquired before our marriage. After fifteen years of marriage, he now says I should reimburse him for that money. I say absolutely not. Who is right?

A It is rarely a simple case of black and white. Contributions made by both parties, including decorating, upkeep supervision, money contributed during the fifteen years, and the amount of money contributed in the beginning are all taken into consideration to determine the overall financial picture at the time of divorce. The increase in the value of the house will be a factor, too; but usually the longer the marriage, the less it matters where the money came from, especially when there are children.

Judy's husband, Rick, was able to prove that he contributed $25,000 to their house down payment from a savings account he had prior to their marriage. Unfortunately this became a major issue in their negotiations, and their lawyers were forced to take it to the judge to rule on. The dollar amount in question was small compared to the cost of the lawyer's fees. In the end the judge decided it was a nonissue, and Rick was not awarded the money because the increased value of the house governed the judge's decision. It is almost always to your advantage to reach an agreement before the judge gets into the matter: When a judge rules you cannot second-guess his decision.

Integrity is the essence of everything successful.
— R. BUCKMINSTER FULLER

Q My husband wants a divorce. We both work, but we live primarily on money inherited from my family. He is insisting that I pay all his expenses and that he continue to live off me and my family. Is that fair?

A This is not a question that has a definitive answer. So much of it hinges on what his financial capabilities are and how he will initially be able to live. Just as women are entitled to receive temporary maintenance to allow them time to rehabilitate themselves, so, too, is your husband. A judge will take into account the overall situation based on the lifestyle you have lived, the length of your marriage, whether children are involved, and how much money your inheritance provides. If you cannot come to a reasonable agreement with your husband, the judge will decide, and he will be guided by a case similar to yours.

Anger makes you smaller, while forgiveness forces you to grow beyond what you were.
— CHÉRIE CARTER-SCOTT

Q I am fifty-eight years old and want to know if I am entitled to Social Security benefits through my ex-spouse when I reach sixty-two.

A The answer is: maybe. There are several criteria you need to meet in order to qualify for Social Security benefits based on your spouse's contributions:

- You were married at least ten years.
- You are at least sixty-two years old.
- You have not remarried.
- Your former spouse is receiving Social Security benefits when you file for divorce.

What Do I Do About Money?

He who rejects change is the architect of decay.
The only human institution which
rejects progress is the cemetery.

—HAROLD WILSON

SIX

HOW CAN I MAKE
THIS EASIER ON MY KIDS?

Minimizing the Divorce's Impact on Your Children

Divorce has as much of an impact on your children as it does on you and your husband, and how well you handle yourself in front of your kids will determine how well they deal with the changes ahead. It's important to think carefully about how you tell your children about the impending divorce—the manner in which they first learn about it will affect their sense of security throughout the coming difficult months. But don't fool yourself into thinking that your divorce will come as a complete surprise to them. In most cases, your children are already aware of your marital difficulties—even when you don't think they've picked up on anything. My clients often mention that when household tensions mount, their children ask if they are getting divorced.

Once you have made the decision to divorce, you and your husband should tell your children together as soon as possible. Stress that the divorce is not their fault, and be sure not to burden them with the details of your problems. This is an important moment to show strength to your children and not be a victim (whether or not it was your husband who asked for the divorce). If you present yourself as a victim you'll make your children feel sorry and guilty for you while unconsciously manipulating their feelings toward their father.

Arguments about visitation are often a stumbling block in many agreements. I don't recommend open-ended visitation schedules because typically they do not benefit anyone. Your divorce agreement should be as specific as possible when it comes to children's issues. It is always easier to set up a schedule at the beginning rather than establishing one later on. The key is to be fair and realize that most parents do want time with their kids, no matter what happened before or during the divorce.

Unfortunately, many people use their children as a weapon in their fight against each other. When issues regarding custody arise between couples, they are often unable to see the harmful impact it has on their children. Your prevailing consideration should always be "What is in the best interests of my children?" Use professionals to assist both of you in making the right decisions.

When Polly came to see me she was in the midst of a divorce after a fifteen-year marriage. She and her husband, Beau, had agreed to see a parenting coordinator to help make some decisions regarding their three adolescent children. The parenting coordinator described co-parenting in a way I will never forget: "Parents are—or should be— the copilots, and their job is to make sure their passengers (their children) have a good flight. The passengers need to know who the copilots are, but they shouldn't be up in the cockpit, and they certainly shouldn't be giving flying instructions. Their job is simply to sit back, relax, and enjoy the ride."

Not long ago Jane came to see me: Danny, her thirteen-year-old son, had recently expressed a desire to live with Nathaniel, his father. Jane felt that Nathaniel, who worked from home and had an unusually flexible schedule, was guilty of manipulating the situation by suggesting that Danny live with him. Nathaniel confided to Danny how lonely he felt and made promises about the adventures they would have together. Danny asked Jane if he could try living with his father.

This was difficult for Jane to accept. We discussed the situation, and I asked Jane several key questions: Why did she think her son was asking to live with his father? Did he want to get to know his father better? Did he feel he had to take care of his father? Was Jane feeling angry toward her husband and refusing to allow the child to express his own preferences? Were there problems at school that her son wanted to escape from, and by moving to his father's could he attend another school? Did her son feel he would receive more material things because his father was wealthy and led a lavish lifestyle? Was his father more permissive?

Since both parents were destined to get into a heated argument, and Nathaniel was threatening a court custody battle, I suggested they consult a child psychologist. Jane said her ex-husband would never consent to that. He didn't, he said, "believe in those people." When their lawyers made it clear to both Jane and Nathaniel that a custody battle could be expensive, time-consuming, and painful—the judge would interview Danny and a mental health professional would be assigned to evaluate all three of them—Nathaniel realized that he was getting in over his head. Both parents ended up consulting a psychologist who was able to help them work out a plan that allowed for equal time with each parent. No longer did Jane feel that Danny's spending more time with Nathaniel was a threat to her position as a mother, and Danny was saved from being placed in the middle of the dispute. The best interests of the child should always be the determinant in the custody decisions.

*Grown-ups never understand anything by themselves,
and it is tiresome for children to be always and
forever explaining things to them.*

— ANTOINE DE SAINT-EXUPÉRY

Q When should I tell my children about our pending divorce, and what should I tell them?

A The amount of information you give your children depends on their ages and their ability to understand the situation. In general I recommend that you:

- Develop a very specific plan for moving ahead as soon as you and your husband agree to begin the divorce procedure—don't put off your decisions.
- Make crystal-clear decisions about where your children will live, where each parent will live, and when one will move out.
- Discuss what kind of visitation schedule will be followed. If it would be helpful, role-play with each other, a therapist, a family member, or a friend.

- Tell your children together. Let them feel that your concerns about them are foremost in your mind. It's important to stress how much you love them and that the breakup is not about them but about your relationship with each other.

- Be specific about how their life will look. Children need a sense of security, a knowledge that you'll both be there for them. Children often blame themselves for the breakup of a marriage, and no matter how much discord children may witness, expect them to be shocked and angry (whether they show it or not). This is not the time to tell them if there is another man or woman in your life.

Bridget's divorce coincided with her teenage daughter Jenny's college application process; soon after she was told about the divorce, Jenny announced that she wasn't going to complete her applications but instead wanted to travel. It was apparent she wanted to run away from the problem. I suggested that Bridget help Jenny get into counseling, so that she could have a place to air her feelings under the guidance of a neutral, compassionate professional. I also suggested that Bridget, along with her husband, consider attending a few sessions with Jenny, either together or apart, to reinforce their mutual concern.

Q What is the difference between physical custody and legal custody?

A Physical custody refers to whom the child lives with. Joint physical custody generally refers to a child who lives in each household half time. Sole physical custody is when the child lives primarily with one parent.

Legal custody refers to who has the decision-making authority for the children when major child-rearing issues (schools, camps, medical issues, therapists, religion, extracurricular lessons, and academic help) are involved. In most divorces, legal custody is held jointly, meaning these decisions are shared by both parents, unless one parent suffers from emotional disorders or is a drug addict, an alcoholic, or a sex offender.

Q My husband doesn't want any custody of our children. What do I do?

A Your husband is going to miss out on a lot, but that is his problem and, of course, your children's problem too. If he doesn't care about your children, perhaps it's better that they don't see him. Honestly, there is nothing you can do, and forcing the situation never works to anyone's advantage.

If life was fair, Elvis would be alive and all the impersonators would be dead.

—JOHNNY CARSON

Q Is a woman in a vulnerable position if she lives separately from her husband and has the children but doesn't file for divorce until the children are grown?

A Believe it or not, many women have asked me this question over the years. I guess that, for some women, the prospect of going through a difficult divorce causes them to envision a scenario—any scenario—that allows them to avoid the confrontation of dissolving their marriage. But let me tell you as forcefully as I can that this is not only a bad idea; it's also a dangerous one.

In the eyes of the law, you are married to your husband and therefore vulnerable to and responsible for anything he may do. You have no legal rights governing your position: If he defaults on bills, incurs debt, or fools with his taxes, you are legally responsible. If he chooses not to give you or your children support, you have no binding agreement to rely on.

The children themselves are another issue: They need clear definition of the situation. The ambiguity of the situation you described is difficult on children. And consider what would happen if one of you falls in love with another person—how could that affect the delicate balance you may (or may not) be able to work out? A separation agreement, with the legal terms of separation clearly defined, gives you a year to see if both of you really want to divorce.

Betty, a stay-at-home mom who was desperate to get back to work and on her own two feet, came to see me in the midst of a very emotionally complicated divorce. She had cheated on her husband, Rob, a decorative painter, and had told him, against my advice, all the lurid details. Rob was so angry he was not able to see what was in anyone's best interests. He stalled at every opportunity and made promises he rarely followed. They agreed that they would split time in the house and the custody of their two sons until they got their finances in order and went to court to finalize their divorce. Betty agreed to stay out of the house during Rob's time, and Rob agreed to stay out of the house during Betty's time with the children. The two biggest problems were that Rob was frequently there when he was not supposed to be, which made Betty furious, often leading to fights in front of the children. Additionally, she was completely dependent upon Rob for money, which he withheld, largely because it was his only weapon. She had no legal document with which to claim her rights. In spite of the fact that there were very small amounts of money in dispute, it was one of the most contentious divorces I have ever seen.

Q Can I get temporary financial support while the details of the divorce are being worked out, and is a judge involved in such a decision?

A Yes, you can get financial support in the midst of a divorce proceeding, and sometimes this issue can be easily agreed upon by the two parties. However, it depends upon the people involved.

Karen and Michael had been married for fifteen years and had a very complicated financial situation. Karen asked for temporary support while the issues of asset evaluation, child support, and visitation were being explored. Asset evaluation can be complicated and take months or even years depending upon how knotty the issues are and the cooperation of the parties involved. Karen was a stay-at-home mom who was financially dependent on her husband, Michael, a contractor. Karen was asked by her lawyer to present a monthly budget that would sustain her and her two children during the divorce proceedings. Since she had never participated in paying the bills, she had to begin from scratch. Together we gathered the information at hand and made estimates about the cost of items we didn't know. At the same time, Michael was preparing his version of the budget, including tax returns. Michael estimated Karen could live on $4,000 a month, while Karen's budget requested $7,000 a month, a large discrepancy that Michael was unwilling to compromise on. It was apparent that Michael wanted to maintain control over her, and money was his method. Since the issue couldn't be resolved by the lawyers, the judge was required to render a decision. Karen was given $6,200 a month. The judge felt this was fair and realistic based on the documents submitted.

Q My husband and I have just started the divorce process. He has accused me, unjustly, of being mentally unstable and an unfit mother. I have been on antidepressants for the past four years, but it's never had an impact on my kids and my depression is under control. What should I do to address his concerns?

A The divorce and legal system encourages frightening and disturbing finger-pointing. Unfortunately, such accusations often cause you to doubt yourself and make you believe that they will impact the outcome of your divorce. My advice: If there are no grounds for the accusations, don't dignify them with a response. Just remember: Your spouse has to prove his accusations. Additionally, responding to a ridiculous accusation only takes time and costs money. Remember that anybody can imply anything, but in a court of law there is a burden of proof. Your lawyer should be adept at fending off any complaints and addressing them if they really do get to a point where they affect the outcome of the trial. Most likely, such an accusation will come to nothing.

Q Do you think children should be forced to go to therapy to deal with a divorce?

A Sometimes. In particularly difficult divorce cases, the court will mandate that the children attend therapy sessions. This isn't really my area of expertise, so I often consult with a trusted therapist who specializes in child psychology when clients come to me with issues about their children during divorce. Her suggestion is to be sure to alert others who come in contact with your children (including teachers and friends' parents) about what's happening in their lives. The other adults in your child's life can help you assess whether there are any changes in their behavior that need professional attention. That said, if your child is resistant to therapy, as many are, most therapists will tell you not to force the issue and not make them go.

Q My children have been going to private school most of their lives, and I want them to continue. My husband does too but says that he will pay up to ten thousand dollars a year in total to cover all expenses not included in child support. This will not begin to cover tuition and will leave me having to pay for about two-thirds of it. My husband makes twice as much money as I do. Is this legal? Fair?

A The question of fairness or legality is not really the issue. What matters is what is in the best interests of the children coupled with the ability to pay. If your children have spent their entire educational life in private schools, to uproot them would not be in their best interest. The divorce itself is enough of a change in circumstances for them to cope with. If the money is available, the court would most likely agree and rule that your husband be required to continue paying. Depending on your income and past history, you too may be required to pay a percentage based on the ratio of your income to his.

Level with your child by being honest.
Nobody spots a phony quicker than a child.
— MARY MacCRACKEN

Q I have custody of my children, and my husband has visitation rights, but I doubt his commitment to my kids in the long term. I'm worried about my will—I don't want him to have custody of them when I die. Do I have any recourse?

A Unless you can prove that he is an unfit father, you have no right to determine a different guardian for your children in the event of your death. And think about it clearly: Is it really in their best interest to live with someone else? I doubt it. I often see clients try to maintain control over each other by using the children as the weapon in their ongoing battles. Once separate and apart, you have no right to control how or what your husband can do with the children. You have grounds for a dispute if his actions are illegal, dangerous, or harmful, but this has to be determined by the court or through the services of a parenting coordinator and not by your personal judgment.

If you tell the truth
you don't have to remember anything.
— MARK TWAIN

Q I know you are not supposed to say bad things about your ex to your children, but recently my ex told my kids a lie and they figured it out. Don't I need to address this? Do I need to let them know that it isn't okay?

A You cannot control the relationship your children have with their father. If they figured out the lie themselves, they'll more than likely continue to figure things out. On the other hand, don't cover for your ex-husband either.

Never forget what a man says to you
when he is angry.

— HENRY WARD BEECHER

Q Can I withhold visitation if my husband isn't pay-ing child support?

A Absolutely, positively not! Even if your ex-husband is a deadbeat dad, child support and visitation rights are two totally separate issues in the eyes of the law. If you withhold visitation, you are in contempt of court. While it may indeed have an adverse effect on your children, missing child support payments is ultimately an issue between you and your ex-husband, not one that involves your kids. It should be handled as such. Whether he pays for their upkeep or not, your ex-husband is still your children's father, and he's an important part of their lives. His inability—or unwillingness—to pay his obligations is something the courts will deal with.

Do not be intimidated by a husband who willfully neglects his obligations. If you are not getting child support payments on time, you can file contempt charges. However, before you can approach the court and file charges, which can subject your ex-husband to jail time, you should exercise some of the other options available to you. It should be noted that each state has slightly different rules, so you should consult a legal professional to learn the specific laws that apply in your state.

The most direct action is to file for a wage deduction order, which takes your support payment directly from his wages. Every state has its own rules on the allowable percentage to deduct, and forms and instructions for filing are available from the family court clerks.

Another method to secure payment is to have the courts compel your husband to post security for future payments. The security could include cash, a bond, or a lien against property. You will have to prove to the court that his defaults have been deliberate and not due to financial problems before the court will impose this method.

When I meet a man I ask myself,
"Is this the man I want my children to spend
their weekends with?"

— RITA RUDNER

Q My husband is on the cusp of getting a new and higher paying job. When his salary increases, will child support/maintenance increase?

A When your divorce is final, your maintenance is determined by your husband's salary at that time. For an increase in salary to affect child support, the increase would have to be substantial (5 percent probably won't be meaningful, whereas 20 percent would be). You should be aware that you have a right to request an increase in child support as a child gets older. However, you should also note that if there is a reversal in your ex-husband's financial situation or a job loss, he too can apply to the court for relief.

Q My husband doesn't want a set parenting schedule; he wants to come and go as he pleases. How
do I enforce a schedule?

A Children thrive on consistency. Every judge will agree
that children need schedules, period. They thrive amid
rules, regulations, and routine. This is why it's so important to know who your husband is and how he is likely
to act during and after your divorce—as well as how you
are likely to act in this same situation. Is he always twenty
minutes late to any appointment? Does he get agitated and
angry if you are five minutes late yourself?

The bottom line: You must have a schedule written into
your agreement, and you need to have a remedy on hand
in case he doesn't keep to it—otherwise you may need to
go back to court. One such remedy is using the services
of a parenting coordinator, which we'll discuss later in this
chapter.

The common schedule used for children of school age
is visitation with the noncustodial parent every other weekend (beginning with dinner on Friday evening and ending
by accompanying them to school on Monday morning),
plus dinner and an overnight visit during the week. On the
other hand, it's good for everyone to have some flexibility,
for your sake as well as for your children's, because as they
get older they will have other activities that require their
time.

Pierre and Beth had been married for twelve years; they had two children and both had very flexible at-home jobs. Pierre often traveled for work, but more important he was the kind of guy who didn't like committing to a schedule—any schedule. He didn't want a visitation schedule; he just wanted their children to come to his house when he was available. He claimed he would be available as much as possible but didn't want to put anything in writing. Beth was adamantly opposed to this—for her own sake as well as for the children's. They could not come to an agreement.

When they went before the judge, he almost laughed at Pierre and said the man had a choice: Either he could make a schedule or the judge would. Pierre agreed to every other weekend and all Tuesdays!

Always remember that the future comes one day at a time.
—DEAN ACHESON

Q My husband, who has traveled and taken jobs in other cities all through our marriage, is threatening to sue for custody of our two daughters. But don't mothers always get custody of children?

A That's not the case nowadays. Today, changing gender roles have changed the traditional rules of custody. Your husband may be using this threat to scare you into agreeing to other concessions you don't want. A parent who travels often for work is not likely to gain primary or sole custody of a minor child. In this case, he may be trying to frighten you into settling for less child support or maintenance.

In general, if the children are very young and both parents work full-time, mothers tend to get primary physical custody. If they are older and can express their own wishes, the court will take their wishes into consideration. Getting involved in a custody battle is a no-win situation. You will be subject to an investigation by court-appointed professionals. Both you and your children will be observed together and apart and asked to appear before the judge. It will surely be traumatic for all. I urge my clients to avoid this at all costs.

Q I've been thinking about getting a divorce, but my kids are so young. Would it be so terrible to wait until they are a bit older?

A No, but staying together doesn't necessarily help the situation either. Too often people use their children as the reason for not proceeding with a divorce. People say they want to "create stability," but the way you and your husband behave toward each other sets the example for your children's future expectations. If the atmosphere in your household is adversarial, your children are certainly aware of that and are negatively impacted. Tension dominates. They are probably hoping the atmosphere will change.

Looking back, Jane realized that it had been hard to get Albert, her seven-year-old son, to stay in bed. Albert would wake up every hour to check up on where Jane and her husband, Samuel, were, often hiding to listen in on their conversations. At school he began fighting with his best friend. It turned out that while Jane was mulling over the situation about her son and delaying filing for divorce, her husband was consulting lawyers and protecting his finances. The problems in their marriage had been going on for more than five years: They were steely with each other, often threatened to divorce, they'd had little or no sex for at least three years, and spent essentially no time either alone or as a family. Shortly after Samuel moved out, Albert began to sleep through the night and also asked if he could have sleepovers. Albert obviously began to feel the tension in the household relax, and he was able to relax as well.

Q Since we separated, my husband has been paying me more than the child support guidelines require. Do voluntary payments set a precedent?

A Voluntary payments above and beyond the support guidelines do not necessarily set a precedent. They are voluntary and just that.

When Sarah, an educator, and Michael, a computer consultant, first separated, she was taking a temporary break from work. They agreed that Michael would pay all the household expenses. For three months he paid almost double what the amount the guidelines suggested and what he ultimately was required to pay in child support. When he realized this, he felt duped, even though he had been in total agreement with this arrangement. Although Sarah and Michael have been divorced for more than four years, whenever the subject of money comes up, he reminds her of this time—the time he sees her as taking advantage of him. The overpayment has not happened again!

You can't have everything. Where would you put it?

— STEVEN WRIGHT

Q **How do you know if you need a parenting coordinator?**

A If you anticipate recurring conflicts around parenting issues, I would advise adding a parenting coordinator clause in your divorce agreement. A parenting coordinator is a trained, neutral person who acts as the child's advocate and helps parents locked in a contentious divorce make child-centered decisions. Pick your parenting coordinator before rather than after problems arise. Parenting coordinators usually ask you to sign a one- to three-year agreement, during which time they cannot be fired unless you both agree. If the judge is aware of the problems the lawyers are having in drawing up an agreement regarding children's issues, sometimes the court will name a parenting coordinator. You agree to split the cost of the coordinator, abide by her decisions, and be cooperative. Parenting coordinators can be lawyers, social workers, or therapists who are familiar with family law, family therapy, and child development.

If your child has a therapist, the parenting coordinator will consult with him to get a better understanding of your child. The issues they deal with concern visitation schedules, protocol for changing dates of visitation, phone call schedules, handling refusals by the child to visit, issues involving extracurricular lessons and sports activities, toys, clothing, etc.

When you are writing up your divorce agreement, you can insert a clause about a parenting coordinator into the agreement, such as: "If the parties have a dispute with respect to parenting schedules or child-rearing issues, they agree to submit the dispute to a parenting coordinator who is empowered to make recommendations in the event the parties are unable to reach agreement. The parenting coordinator's recommendations shall be binding, subject to judicial review." The more details regarding parental responsibilities you build into your divorce agreement, the less conflict the children will be exposed to, and the less often the coordinator will be called in to mediate.

Q My lawyer suggests that we have a parenting coordinator. Is it necessary to determine who the person is at the time we sign the papers, or can we just find one if we ever need one?

A Hire a parenting coordinator before you file your agreement. My advice to all my clients is to get as much as possible written into your agreement before you sign it. If you're still feeling angry with each other, trying to enforce something after the fact takes time, money, and effort. In reality the anger remains with you for a long time, and for some it never really goes away.

Keri had a parenting coordinator clause written into her agreement but didn't select a coordinator prior to signing it. About a year after the divorce, she wanted to invoke this clause and suggested to her ex-husband, Pat, that they choose one. Not only did Pat not want to do this, he did everything possible to halt the process. First he said he wouldn't go see a woman (he felt a woman would be too sympathetic to Keri), and second he went beyond their agreed-upon group of three coordinators to choose from and selected five. Keri began to feel she would need a parenting coordinator to choose how to choose a parenting coordinator. Luckily no one charged for the interview process, but it was time wasted that could have been avoided if they had selected the coordinator prior to their troubles.

Q If I work will I have any responsibilities for child support? How are child support numbers determined?

A Child support payments are generally apportioned between both parents if they both work. As a rule, the courts take the gross income of the two individuals, subtract Social Security income tax payments, mandatory retirement contributions, preexisting spousal and child support obligations (for example, support payments from another marriage), and other specific expenses, to come up with the spouses' net income. You should note that some states use gross income for calculating child support; you'll have to consult with your lawyer to determine which method your state uses.

John and Kathy have two children and reside in New York State, which uses the net income rule. The Child Support Standards Act (CSSA) states that 25 percent of the combined income be provided in support for two children. They have a combined net income of $85,000 (John makes $60,000 as an engineer and Kathy makes $25,000 as a secretary); therefore the required support for the children would total $21,250 a year. John's share is 70 percent ($60,000 divided by $85,000) and Kathy's is 30 percent ($25,000 divided by $85,000). According to this formula, John contributes $14,875 and Kathy $6,375. Since Kathy has primary physical custody, John pays Kathy $14,875 per year, or $1,239.58 per month.

Q My husband has just filed for bankruptcy. Does this affect his child support obligation?

A Child support obligations are not eliminated due to bankruptcy; however, if bankruptcy affects your husband's financial situation, he would be entitled to a reduction in future support payments.

Q I'm recently separated, and my eight-year-old son doesn't want to stay at his father's house. Every time he goes there he calls me to get him and take him home, and I pick him up. Should I make him stay?

A Yes and no. Different people have different opinions about this situation. Some people feel that you should force a child to go, and others are more likely to take into account the child's personality: Does he have separation anxiety? Is he change averse? Is he going to spend his time at his father's house completely miserable? This is a problem that you may have to deal with by getting help from a therapist. I don't think most lawyers or divorce coaches would want to weigh in on this—and honestly, I don't think they should.

Q What items does child support cover and what items are considered extras?

A Child support covers the expenses for your children to live in your household, including lodging, transportation, food, clothing, allowance, books, entertainment, child care, sports equipment, and incidentals such as haircuts, toiletries, birthday gifts, toys, bedroom

What Your Divorce Lawyer May Not Tell You

furniture. The "extras" cover school tuition, lessons, after-school activities, health insurance, unreimbursed medical expenses, college tuition, and expenses at school if the child is living away from home. Generally, when a child goes to college and lives away from home, the amount of child support payments is reduced; this should be stipulated in your divorce agreement. In some states it can remain the same unless one party files for a modification. If possible, have your husband be responsible for paying the "extras" directly, so that he'll be responsible when they increase, and if he's late in paying them, creditors will go after him rather than you.

Q My husband has been out of the house for about a year. He has had several girlfriends and now wants to introduce a new one to the kids. I know they will just break up and don't want my kids involved. Do you think I am right?

A I know it's hard to hear this—but no, I don't. Unfortunately (or maybe fortunately), you have no control over what your ex-husband does. You have no right to dictate what he can or cannot do. You are leading independent lives now, and while you can offer advice if it is truly in the best interests of your children, he has no obligation to listen to or follow it.

Q We have raised our children in the Catholic Church in spite of the fact that my ex-husband is Jewish. He has started taking my son to his synagogue and I am outraged. Can I stop him?

A This issue of what religion the children will be raised in should be defined in your divorce agreement. Taking your son to temple doesn't constitute converting him. In fact, it gives your son an overview of what his father's traditions are about, which is part of his own heritage.

Q I have to admit it: I am mad and feel like retaliating at my ex-husband. I don't want to allow him to switch weekends so that he can be with his girlfriend (who broke up our marriage). Do you think I should switch?

A Your rule of thumb is always based on the answer to this question: What is in the best interests of the children? So try to put aside your anger and ask yourself: Do your children want to be with him and look forward to it? Is it inconvenient for you to switch weekends or is your anger the determining factor? As life goes on, there may be other people in your life too. What if you need to change your schedule in the future?

I know this isn't always easy, but try to get beyond the girlfriend or any other extraneous circumstances and think of your children first. Bobbi, a school superintendent and mother of two, had been separated about two years when she came to see me. Her husband, George, a financial advisor, was enjoying his life as a single man—dare I say playboy—and went from girlfriend to girlfriend. He was constantly changing his schedule to accommodate his dates. It drove Bobbi wild, and in truth she didn't feel that it was good for their kids. At first she said yes every time he asked, but eventually she took the children for him during his time but would not trade so he lost time with his children. She was a bit more rigid than necessary, but it sent a message to George, who eventually understood: If he wanted to see his kids, he had to commit to them!

Q During my husband's weekends with the kids, he often travels and leaves the children with his mother. Is this right?

A Since she is a member of your children's family, it doesn't constitute abandonment. As long as they are having a great time with her, I approve. Again, your rule of thumb is always based on the answer to this question: What is in the best interests of the children?

Boris was a chef with restaurants in several cities. His wife, Dorothea, was a stay-at-home mom but really cherished her weekends without her kids so she could spend time with her boyfriend. Boris's mother was local and would go to Boris's apartment to stay with the kids when he wasn't in town. Dorothea really wanted Boris to be with the kids, but since it worked for her—and the kids loved it—she couldn't really complain.

Q My husband never pays his bills on time, and I'm dependent on the money. What happens if my child support is always late?

A I hear this all the time from women—they complain that their ex-husband uses late payment of their monthly child support as a way to needle them, but he eventually pays by the end of the month. If he is a traditional late payer and did so throughout your marriage (with bills), I advise you to negotiate for your divorce agreement to allow you to have his wages garnished on a monthly basis. Generally people do not like their employers to know their personal business, so this threat could become a way of making him comply promptly with his obligation. Another slightly less drastic option: Ask him to set up an automatic bank deposit every payday that deposits the amount directly into your checking account—this negates the "check is in the mail" excuse. The rules and regulations vary by state, so be sure to get clarification from your lawyer.

Q My ex-husband says he's entitled to deduct the children on his taxes because he pays child support. Is this true?

A No. The tax benefit depends on the income level of both parents and generally should go to the parent with the greatest tax benefit, provided that parent is providing some support. As a rule, if there are two children, each parent gets one exemption unless it is more or less beneficial for one parent to get both. For more information, I would advise you to talk with an accountant.

It is better to be hated for what you are than to be loved for what you are not.

—ANDRÉ GIDE

Q How are child support payments protected if my ex-husband dies before my children reach emancipation? How will I manage to pay for their day-to-day expenses and their college tuition?

A Most divorce agreements require that your husband purchase a life insurance policy, in which you would be named beneficiary, that is large enough to cover support payments and college tuition. Each year, as your child nears emancipation, your husband is entitled to reduce the proceeds of the policy to equal his remaining liability.

A high station in life is earned by the gallantry with which appalling experiences are survived with grace.

—TENNESSEE WILLIAMS

Q My mother set up a trust to pay for my children's private school education (including nursery school, etc.) I was married only two years, and my husband doesn't know about the trust. When my daughter goes to school, must I use all the money, or can I ask him to pay for half?

A It is important to be honest about your financial situation. You may be right to think your husband knows nothing about the trust, but you're taking a chance. If he becomes aware of it after you've signed your agreement, your child support payment, as well as your honesty, could come into question. If your ex-husband chooses to reopen your case, you would have return to court, where he would receive an adjustment in his obligation. Additionally, the court might order you to reimburse him for the over-charges.

People change and forget to tell each other.

— LILLIAN HELLMAN

SEVEN

MY HUSBAND LOOKED UP
WHAT ONLINE?

Divorcing in the Internet Age

The divorce courts are still creating rules governing spouses' online transactions during a divorce. The Internet is a wonderful and efficient way to look for information on divorce (and everything else), check out attorneys, and exchange information in divorce chat rooms. Several of my clients have mentioned that they are able to access information about their spouses through e-mail or the Web that gives insight into their estranged spouse's activities. At this time no rules have been created regarding whether it's legal (never mind ethical) to use the information obtained in this way.

I recently read about ex-wives who use blogs to tell

their side of the marital saga. It's a soap opera of true confessions. In one such case a husband sued his wife, claiming that her writings were both obnoxious and offensive and violated the terms of their divorce settlement. However, a justice of the Supreme Court of the State of New York ruled that the husband had no grounds for his claims and upheld his wife's rights based on the First Amendment. Today, some lawyers include confidentiality provisions in their agreements that forbid either party to reveal things about the marriage.

Q There are many online sites for do-it-yourself divorces. Do you approve?

A I wouldn't trust an online divorce unless it's for a short marriage with no children and no complicated financial obligations: There are just too many issues—both big and small—that will require guidance from someone with a lot of experience. Online sites can be helpful in giving you an overview of the process, but at this point divorce via the Internet is not a solution I recommend.

There are many other good sources of information, such as the bar association in your city, which can help with free advice, as can your local courthouse, where you can find pro bono lawyers who are available to guide you through the process. Pro bono lawyers are usually available only if you do not have enough income to afford a lawyer. Don't count on the clerks: While some of them are incredibly friendly and even helpful, they are not supposed to dispense advice, and truthfully, they are not qualified to do so.

Q My husband and I are in the process of getting divorced, but before we broke up I set up our credit cards so that I could access them online. He doesn't know and hasn't changed any of his passwords—and I can't resist looking to see where he's spending his money now that we are apart. Do you think it's okay to spy like this?

A If you can get to the information without giving yourself away, I'm not against it. However always keep your lawyer informed of what you are doing. You are, in fact, entitled to see all his financial documentation, including credit card statements, expense accounts, bank accounts, loan statements, etc., and he is entitled to see all of yours. If either of you are not cooperative, the judge will require the documents to be produced.

Magda learned a lot about her husband, Edward, when she used his computer when hers was being repaired. His e-mails showed correspondence with several women whom he was obviously seeing on his numerous business trips. She immediately confronted him about her discovery, and he begged and even cried for her forgiveness. He loved her and thought nothing about these women. They were one-night stands and he would reform. In the meantime, Magda had copied all the e-mails for a period of three years and put them away in a safety deposit box. She warned him that if she discovered anything else, the marriage was over.

For the next six months he was on his best behavior, more attentive and more giving than ever before. But Magda was still on her guard. She went to California to visit her family and asked her best friend and neighbor to keep an eye on Edward while she was gone. During her absence, her neighbor saw Edward in the garden kissing a woman. Magda was immediately informed but kept quiet. As soon as she returned she went back to his computer for information only to discover a photograph of a woman posing on a bed. Upon further investigation she realized the bed was . . . yes, you guessed it, her bed.

She confronted Edward with the garden scene but didn't mention the photograph. This she would save in case she needed it. He told her how sorry he was and how he had a problem with needing more than one woman to satisfy his needs. Magda was the only one he loved and he would do anything for her. For Magda it was totally over: She felt violated and knew she couldn't trust him. She began to realize he was a manipulative liar whom she couldn't tolerate. I told her if he was really feeling guilty this was the time to take action. His guilt could make it easier for her to get what she felt she deserved. My advice: Strike while the iron is hot.

Q I caught my husband having an affair because he left some things on our computer: a map to her house, plane reservations. I started to look further and have found e-mails to her for the past five years. He has been taking trips with this woman when I thought he was away on business. What do I do with the information?

A This information could help provide grounds for adultery, but it doesn't necessarily affect the financial outcome of your divorce, unless he's using family assets to provide his entertainment and denying your family their rightful support.

When Lisa, a schoolteacher, called me she had just discovered very damning evidence about David, her husband. The things she found on her computer clearly indicated that he had been having an affair. Every time she found something she dug deeper. Frankly, she was beside herself. While I don't blame her for satisfying her curiosity, in terms of the outcome of her divorce, it made no difference. David was clearly a liar and a cheat, but that had no impact on either their financial or custody decisions.

Q I don't like speaking to my husband. Would e-mails be an appropriate way to communicate with him?

A Yes, but remember that you leave a wide wake behind—any e-mail you write can be brought back later in your divorce proceedings as evidence. Be conscious of the tone you use and the things that you commit to the correspondence. E-mails can often prove conversations that you may or may not wish you'd had. Paper disintegrates or gets lost: E-mail is forever. Don't write anything in e-mail that you wouldn't want to hear read aloud in a court of law—because that's just what could happen.

Q **My husband sent me an e-mail committing to sharing all expenses related to upkeep on the house until our divorce was finalized. He is now refusing and saying he agreed to no such thing. Can I use a copy of the e-mail as evidence?**

A Yes, you can. E-mail shows intent but does not constitute an agreement. Remember, there is no agreement until there is an actual agreement; whether he said it either in writing or verbally, he can change his mind. Nothing is enforceable unless it is in the divorce agreement.

The difficulty with marriage is that we fall in love with a personality, but must live with a character.
— PETER DE VRIES

Q I found my husband looking at child pornography on the Internet. He claims it's the first time, but I'm just sickened. I threw him out that night and started searching his Internet history. I came up with the vilest stuff imaginable. Do I report him? Do I allow him to see our children?

A You must report this to your lawyer or mediator immediately because child pornography is illegal. This could become a huge issue and will certainly impact his ability to have joint custody of the children.

However, if it's adult pornography, nobody will think twice about it. And while you can bring it up as a concern, the feeling of the court is basically that if it's a private computer and not easily available to the children, it's okay. As long as the children aren't exposed, the adult has his rights.

Not too long ago my client, Betty, a smart politician, discovered she had access to her real estate investor husband's computer and could readily snoop on what he was doing and whom he was e-mailing. To her surprise and shock Dan was spending an inordinate amount of time on adult pornography sites costing several hundred dollars a month. She also discovered that he was having an affair with their babysitter. This made her both sick to her stomach and furious.

Not surprisingly, her rage turned to a desire for vengeance. The children, boys ages ten and thirteen, she decided, would be used for her purposes: Betty's intent was to file for sole custody of the children and deny Dan any and all visitation rights. I suggested she think twice about this because a trial would take place and the matter would be fully investigated. More important, her children would be drawn into the divorce procedures. Experts would be involved in determining the relationships the children had with each parent. It would be messy! But Betty was determined and couldn't be stopped. She even fired her lawyer because he disagreed with her plan; she simply hired another. In the end, Dan's pornography habit was not judged to be an impediment to his good parenting—and while Betty was given legal custody (the sole right to determine her children's future), she was not successful in denying Dan visitation. The jury is out on how contact with their father and the exposure to the trial ordeal will impact the two children.

Q I have a single friend who has been doing some Internet dating. My husband and I are not gloriously happy, but we haven't been talking about divorce. She recently found my husband on one of the sites. What do I do?

A It's time you confront the situation you're living in. Clearly, neither of you is happy, and it's possible he's already getting his life and finances in order. Start taking notice and get prepared with financial information. Learn your rights. "Preparation is protection" is my best advice to my clients.

CONCLUSION

LIFE AFTER DIVORCE

Women often ask me how long it will take to truly get on their feet and move forward after a divorce. Of all the questions in this book, that one may be the most difficult to answer. I've heard many people say that a divorce takes two years to recover from. Others say it takes half as many years as you were married—a depressing prospect for those of us ending long-term relationships!

The truth is that the healing process depends on many factors, including how good you feel about yourself, whether the hurt and pain have subsided, and if you have been able to move on from your relationship and meet new people to fill your life. Some women find that their friends absolutely save them during this tough time. Others will have to seek out new friends, as they discover that the married couples they used to see will no longer remain close. Unfortunately, many married women choose to break off their relationships with divorced women, worried that the same could happen to them—or even because they are envious of their newly single friend. Look at divorce as an opportunity to make new friends and participate in new activities. Sometimes it's a chance to renew your interest in things you love to do but didn't because your husband didn't share your interests.

It's helpful to redefine who you are and understand what went wrong and how you played a part in your divorce. Be careful about repeating the same familiar mistakes. Take time out for therapy. Reestablish your own self-esteem and self-worth. Get comfortable with your new independence. Don't feel you have to date; you may discover that you neither need nor want to have another person around all the time. Then again, you may enjoy getting back into the dating scene again.

If you have children, this is a good time to explore how you will handle your position as a single parent. Focus your attention on spending quality time with them. Even if you're working all day, time together should be quality time. Cook dinner together regularly and plan household chores, like raking leaves, together. Don't schedule phone calls or visits from your friends during this time. Make bedtime a quiet and peaceful time to connect, especially if your children are young. As time moves on, I promise you: It will get easier and easier.

As your children get older and more independent, you will all adjust. You will surely feel mixed emotions, as will your children, about single parenting. Sometimes you'll be angry, overwhelmed, and drained; other times your children will infuse you with joy and energy and provide an amazing support system. There are several realities you should recognize about parenting, especially single parenting and the effects of divorce on children. The whole process isn't easy, and no book can give you all the answers. Making your own life positive will have an enormous impact on your children. The way you handle the stress and setbacks in your life will allow you to become a role model for your children. Don't ever think of yourself as a victim or someone who has been used and abused. Do everything you can not to involve your children in the issues you have with your former husband. Encourage your kids' relationship with their father. It will reward you in the end. With a healthy parent-child relationship, your children will function as solid citizens able to lead happy adult lives.

Do some self-discovery. Think about counseling. Many of our behavior patterns are learned during childhood and often unconsciously seep into our adult lives. Some of this behavior may have affected your marriage. Now is the time to examine and learn about them before you repeat them.

Learning about yourself is always helpful. How often have you met someone's second spouse and thought how much like the first he appears to be? He's not different; he's just newer! It's easy to pick the familiar and much harder to take the time to explore ourselves.

Most important, learn to treat yourself well. Karen took up skiing with her kids. Helayne bought herself an automatic car starter so on cold winter days she could get into a warm car. Mary could finally cover the couches in the living room with the fabric she'd always wanted. This is your time, and remember that amid all the craziness swirling around you, you need and deserve to be happy.

After my own divorce, my life took on new meaning. I regained my strength, my security, my confidence, my comfort in my own skin, and a faith in the future—my future. Life was no longer dependent on accommodating my husband; instead, I focused on making myself—and my children—happy and fulfilled. I was ready for what was next in my life.

For me, divorce was a chance at a new beginning, not an ending. Think positively as you move forward. Understand that you may have made a mistake, but you are human and not alone.

GLOSSARY OF
COMMON LEGAL TERMS
IN A DIVORCE

A

Action: A lawsuit that goes to court.

Addendum: An addition to an original document.

Agreement: A formal written understanding between two parties about their rights and duties to each other. The agreement needs to be signed by both parties to make it binding.

Answer: A response to a complaint.

Attachment: A court order that seizes a debtor's property and transfers it to the person to whom the debt is owed.

B

Burden of proof: A party's duty to prove claims in the lawsuit.

C

Caption: Appears at the top of a paper filing for a motion or pleading that shows the names of the plaintiff and defendant, the name of the court, the court part, and the index number that is assigned throughout the procedure.

Child support: The money paid by the noncustodial parent to the custodial parent to cover a child's expenses after separation and/or divorce.

Child Support Standards Act (CSSA): The name of the law that determines child support obligation. The support rules differ by state.

Clerk: A court official who handles materials such as filings and motions.

COBRA (Consolidated Omnibus Budget Reconciliation Act): A law passed by Congress that provides group health insurance coverage to someone who might otherwise have it terminated.

Complaint: The initial document presented by the plaintiff or his/her attorney. In a divorce, it contains the plaintiff's reasons for divorce.

Contempt: The willful disregard of a judge's court order.

Contested divorce: A divorce action that is opposed by the defendant spouse.

Cruel and inhuman treatment: One of the reasons for beginning divorce. The treatment refers to cruelty—whether physical, verbal, sexual, or emotional—committed by the defendant against the plaintiff that can endanger the plaintiff's physical or mental self. It makes living together impossible.

Custody, legal: The legal right to make all decisions affecting a child under the age of emancipation, which varies by state.

Custody, physical: The actual physical care and primary residence of a child under the age of emancipation.

D

Defendant: The person who is served with the divorce papers.

Deposition: A person's out-of-court, sworn testimony for use in the lawsuit. It is conducted in a manner similar to trial, although a judge is not present. Another name for deposition is examination before trial (EBT).

Discovery: A party's request for disclosure of information, usually financial, to be used in a divorce action.

E

Emancipation: A child's release from the responsibility and control of a parent or guardian. The age varies by state.

Equitable distribution: The method that marital property and assets are divided by the law in a divorce action. Equitable distribution does not necessarily mean a 50 percent split. Distribution is based on various factors presented to the court. Equitable means fair, not equal.

Evidence: Testimony, documents, or tangible objects that are used to prove or disprove accusations.

Exhibit: A document, record, or other tangible object introduced as evidence in court.

Expert: A person who is considered an authority on a particular subject. Experts are often used in helping the judge in making a decision.

F

Family court: The place where judges hear cases and issues orders involving child support, custody, visitation, spousal support, and family offenses.

G

Grounds: Legally sufficient reason for granting divorce.

Guardian ad litem: Usually a lawyer or therapist appointed by the court to help a minor or incompetent person in a divorce. The guardian ad litem does not act as a lawyer for the child but reports to the court on what is in the child's best interests.

I

Index number: The number assigned to a case by the court. The number is used on all papers served on the parties and filed with the court.

Glossary

Interrogatory: A set of questions given to the parties in the a lawsuit that have to be answered.

J

Judgment of divorce: The document issued and signed by the court granting the divorce.

L

Law guardian: A court-appointed lawyer for the child in contested custody matters.

M

Maintenance: The name for spousal support, also known as "alimony."

Marital property: Property and assets that the plaintiff or defendant obtained during the marriage. These include items such as a house, car, IRA, bank account, pension, annuity, business, and advanced degree. However, certain items, such as an inheritance, a gift from someone other than your spouse, or compensation for personal injuries, may be deemed by the court to be separate property.

O

Order: A court direction. Failure to follow can result in contempt of court.

Order of protection: An order from the court that directs one person to stop certain conduct against another person. This order can exclude a person from the residence, ordering him to stay away from the other person or their children.

P

Plaintiff: The person who starts the divorce action.

Postnuptial: A contract, same as a prenuptial, only signed after the marriage takes place.

Prenuptial: A written contract that establishes a couple's rights in case of death or divorce. This agreement is entered into prior to a marriage.

S

Separate property: Property the court considers to belong only to one spouse or the other. It is not part of equitable distribution.

Separation agreement: A written contract concerning issues of child support, spousal payments, division of marital property, debts and bills, responsibilities for residence and children care, plus visitation rights. It requires the signatures of both parties.

Spouse: Husband or wife.

Stipulation: A voluntary agreement between parties on issues related to the divorce.

Subpoena: A court order requesting a person's attendance at a time and place to testify as a witness or to provide certain documents that are requested. Failure to comply can result in a citation for contempt of court.

Support: Payment for housing, food, clothing, and other living expenses.

U

Uncontested divorce: A divorce action in which the defendant agrees not to oppose the divorce.

V

Visitation: The right of a noncustodial parent to be with a child.

W

Waiver: Willingly giving up rights or claims.